CONVERSATIONS
WITH SCRIPTURE:
THE BOOK
OF DANIEL

Other Books in the Series

CONVERSATIONS
WITH SCRIPTURE:

THE BOOK
OF DANIEL

EDMOND F. DESUEZA
AND JUDITH JONES

Morehouse Publishing
NEW YORK · HARRISBURG · DENVER

To our children

"Against wisdom evil does not prevail."
—WISDOM OF SOLOMON 7:30

Morehouse Publishing, 4775 Linglestown Road, Harrisburg, PA 17112

Morehouse Publishing, 445 Fifth Avenue, New York, NY 10016

Morehouse Publishing is an imprint of Church Publishing Incorporated.

Cover art: 5th century A.D., Tunisia, Tunis, Musee National Du Bardo (Archaeological Museum), Early Christian; credit: DEA / G. DAGLI ORTI

Series cover design by Corey Kent

Series design by Beth Oberholtzer

Library of Congress Cataloging-in-Publication Data

Desueza, Edmond F.
    Conversations with Scripture : the book of Daniel / Edmond F. Desueza and Judith Jones.
        p.   cm.
    Includes bibliographical references (p.   ) and index.
    ISBN 978-0-8192-2409-5 (pbk. : alk. paper)
    ISBN 978-0-8192-2750-8 (ebook)
    1. Bible. O.T. Daniel—Criticism, interpretation, etc.   I. Jones, Judith. II. Title.
BS1555.52.D47   2011
224'.506—dc23
                                                                    2011029632

Printed in the United States of America

10 9 8 7 6 5 4 3 2 1

CONTENTS

Almighty God, who created us in your own image:
Grant us grace fearlessly to contend against evil and
to make no peace with oppression; and, that we may
reverently use our freedom, help us to employ it in the
maintenance of justice in our communities and among
the nations, to the glory of your holy Name; through
Jesus Christ our Lord, who lives and reigns with you
and the Holy Spirit, one God, now and for ever.

AMEN.

Sovereign God, you invite us to contemplate your
presence in the whole creation: give us wisdom to
understand you as you are revealed in all generations,
languages, and cultures, grant us grace to see you at
work in every person, and inspire us to do your will,
glorify your name and offer you worship, through your
Son Jesus Christ, the Lord of history from age to age.

AMEN.

INTRODUCTION
TO THE SERIES

To talk about a distinctively Anglican approach to Scripture is a daunting task. Within any one part of the larger church that we call the Anglican Communion there is, on historical grounds alone, an enormous variety. But as the global character of the church becomes apparent in ever-newer ways, the task of accounting for that variety, while naming the characteristics of a distinctive approach becomes increasingly difficult.

In addition, the examination of Scripture is not confined to formal studies of the kind addressed in this series of parish studies written by formally trained biblical scholars. Systematic theologian David Ford, who participated in the Lambeth Conference of 1998, rightly noted that although "most of us have studied the Bible over many years" and "are aware of various academic approaches to it," we have "also lived in it" and "inhabited it, through worship, preaching, teaching and meditation." As such, Ford observes, "The Bible in the Church is like a city we have lived in for a long time." We may not be able to account for the history of every building or the architecture on every street, but we know our way around and it is a source of life to each of us.[1]

That said, we have not done as much as we should in acquainting the inhabitants of that famed city with the architecture that lies within. So, as risky as it may seem, it is important to set out an introduction to the highlights of that city—which this series proposes to explore at length. Perhaps the best way in which to broach that task is to provide a handful of descriptors.

The first of those descriptors that leaps to mind is familiar, basic, and forever debated: *authoritative.* Years ago I was asked by a colleague who belonged to the Evangelical Free Church why someone with as much obvious interest in the Bible would be an Episcopal priest. I responded, "Because we read the whole of Scripture and not just the parts of it that suit us." Scripture has been and continues to play a singular role in the life of the Anglican Communion, but it has rarely been used in the sharply prescriptive fashion that has characterized some traditions.

Some have characterized this approach as an attempt to navigate a *via media* between overbearing control and an absence of accountability. But I think it is far more helpful to describe the tensions not as a matter of steering a course between two different and competing priorities, but as the complex dance necessary to live under a very different, but typically Anglican notion of authority itself. Authority shares the same root as the word "to author" and as such, refers first and foremost, not to the *power* to *control* with all that both of those words suggest, but to the capacity to *author creativity*, with all that both of those words suggest.[2] As such, the function of Scripture is to carve out a creative space in which the work of the Holy Spirit can yield the very kind of fruit associated with its work in the Church. The difficulty, of course, is that for that space to be creative, it is also necessary for it to have boundaries, much like the boundaries we establish for other kinds of genuinely creative freedom—the practice of scales for concert pianists, the discipline of work at the barré that frees the ballerina, or the guidance that parents provide for their children. Defined in this way, it is possible to see the boundaries around that creative space as barriers to be eliminated, or as walls that provide protection, but they are neither.

And so the struggle continues with the authority of Scripture. From time to time in the Anglican Communion, it has been and will be treated as a wall that protects us from the complexity of navigating without error the world in which we live. At other times, it will be treated as the ancient remains of a city to be cleared away in favor of a brave new world. But both approaches are rooted, not in the limitations of Scripture, but in our failure to welcome the creative space we have been given.

For that reason, at their best, Anglican approaches to Scripture are also *illuminative*. William Sloane Coffin once observed that the problem with Americans and the Bible is that we read it like a drunk uses a lamppost. We lean on it, we don't use it for illumination.[3] Leaning on Scripture—or having the lamppost taken out completely—are simply two very closely related ways of failing to acknowledge the creative space provided by Scripture. But once the creative space is recognized for what it is, then the importance of reading Scripture illuminatively becomes apparent. Application of the insight Scripture provides into who we are and what we might become is not something that can be prescribed or mapped out in detail. It is only a conversation with Scripture, marked by humility that can begin to spell out the particulars. Reading Scripture is, then, in the Anglican tradition a delicate and demanding task, that involves both the careful listening for the voice of God and courageous conversation with the world around us.

It is, for that reason, an approach that is also marked by *critical engagement* with the text itself. It is no accident that from 1860 to 1900 the three best-known names in the world of biblical scholarship were Anglican priests, the first two of whom were Bishops: B. F. Westcott, J. B. Lightfoot, and F. J. A. Hort. Together the three made contributions to both the church and the critical study of the biblical text that became a defining characteristic of Anglican life.

Of the three, Westcott's contribution, perhaps, best captures the balance. Not only did his work contribute to a critical text of the Greek New Testament that would eventually serve as the basis for the English Revised Version, but as Bishop of Durham he also convened a conference of Christians to discuss the arms race in Europe, founded the Christian Social Union, and mediated the Durham coal strike of 1892.

The English roots of the tradition are not the only, or even the defining characteristic of Anglican approaches to Scripture. The church, no less than the rest of the world, has been forever changed by the process of globalization, which has yielded a rich *diversity* that complements the traditions once identified with the church.

Scripture in Uganda, for example, has been read with an emphasis on private, allegorical, and revivalist applications. The result has been a tradition in large parts of East Africa that stresses the reading of Scripture on one's own; the direct application made to the contemporary situation without reference to the setting of the original text; and the combination of personal testimony with the power of public exhortation.

At the same time, however, globalization has brought that tradition into conversation with people from other parts of the Anglican Communion as the church in Uganda has sought to bring the biblical text to bear on its efforts to address the issues of justice, poverty, war, disease, food shortage, and education. In such a dynamic environment, the only thing that one can say with certainty is that neither the Anglican Communion, nor the churches of East Africa, will ever be the same again.

Authoritative, illuminative, critical, and varied—these are not the labels that one uses to carve out an approach to Scripture that can be predicted with any kind of certainty. Indeed, if the word *dynamic*—just used—is added to the list, perhaps all that one can predict is still more change! And, for that reason, there will be observers who (not without reason) will argue that the single common denominator in this series is that each of the authors also happens to be an Anglican. (There might even be a few who will dispute that!)

But such is the nature of life in any city, including one shaped by the Bible. We influence the shape of its life, but we are also shaped and nurtured by it. And if that city is of God's making, then to force our own design on the streets and buildings around us is to disregard the design that the chief architect has in mind.

—Frederick W. Schmidt
Series Editor

AUTOBIOGRAPHICAL NOTE

Edmond: I am a cradle Episcopalian, born and raised in a rural area in the Dominican Republic where my father worked in the sugar cane industry. Although I was confirmed in the Episcopal Church, as a young man I distanced myself from my religious upbringing and for six years did not attend church at all. Eventually, however, other Episcopal youth and the priests who worked with them drew me back into church life. At first I read the Bible only in places that seemed sacred to me, accepting everything that it said without question. In seminary it came as a great shock to me that the Bible can be read anywhere and that it can be interpreted in a variety of ways. After I was ordained, my first assignments were in the sugar cane growing regions of the Dominican Republic, where at times I was responsible for congregations in six different communities at once. During those years when I worked among the rural poor, I focused on Isaiah and Amos because they stress both social and divine justice. Later, as I studied Leviticus, Revelation, and Daniel, with their emphasis on social issues and the dream of a world made new, I began to perceive that religion was inseparably connected with culture, anthropology, and economics. I live entranced by life in all its rich diversity, but fascinated above all by human beings and their emerging purpose in the cosmos. The scriptures are for me like an enormous ocean where, when I cast out my line, I discover chaos and life, human nature with all its imperfection and promise, and the vision of a God who is both nearer than our breath and beyond our understanding.

Judith: I was born in India to parents who were medical missionaries in the Church of the Nazarene. My earliest memories revolve around church life: sitting cross-legged on the floor of the church, singing hymns in Marathi; being awakened before dawn on Christmas day by carolers whom we welcomed with hot tea and doughnuts; and hiding inside a cardboard box on our veranda, teaching myself to read by puzzling out the words of Bible storybooks. Intermingled with those happy memories are vivid images of desperate poverty—stick-thin men and women, children with stomachs distended from malnutrition, and the crowded slums of Mumbai and Calcutta. When I was nine, my family moved to central California, and the local Nazarene church embraced us. Although biblical characters, concepts, and language continued to permeate my daily life, I heard little concern for the human needs in our community. At the Nazarene College I attended, however, my professors introduced me to the social emphasis of biblical law and to the prophets' call to do justice. They challenged me to read the Bible critically and taught me that asking hard questions can deepen faith. During graduate school I found my home in the Episcopal Church, where the liturgy emphasizes a central scriptural message: love for God is inseparable from love for neighbor, and God's kingdom comes on earth as well as in heaven. Scripture draws us back to God, and God sends us out into the world.

The Kingdom, the Power, and the Glory

For many Christians, the book of Daniel is both very familiar and very strange. It opens with stories that many of us learned in childhood, such as Daniel in the lion's den, the Hebrew children in the fiery furnace, and the handwriting on the wall. In the second half of Daniel, however, we encounter a strange new world inhabited by angelic beings and many-horned beasts, goats and rams and armies at war. In some ways the book of Daniel itself is an odd animal, a hybrid collection of court tales and strange visions, written in two different languages, Hebrew and Aramaic, with some parts that are as engaging as a child's bedtime story and others that are mystifying and difficult even for adults.

The familiar stories at the beginning of Daniel have often been treated as if they were tales with a simple moral: remain faithful, and God will rescue you even from the lion's mouth. If we are honest with ourselves, however, such simplicity does not mesh well with history and with our own experience of reality, for we know that sometimes the children of God have been fed to the lions and God has not intervened. Sometimes the children of God have been thrown into the furnace and have not emerged unscathed;

sometimes the feasting continues unabated, and the powerful live on, oblivious to the handwriting on the wall. Can the stories in Daniel speak to such a world, or are they tales meant only for children?

And what about the series of visions at the end of Daniel? As interpreted by popular authors such as Hal Lindsay in *The Late Great Planet Earth* and, more recently, Tim LaHaye and Jerry B. Jenkins in the best-selling *Left Behind* series, the visions are a description of the end of the world. And since, according to these authors, the end of the world is imminent, Daniel's visions are simply a code language for events and characters in our own day. Certainly in an age of climate change and missing nuclear materials there is reason to take seriously the possibility that we are facing the destruction of the world as we know it. Yet by understanding Daniel's visions as a message written directly for us, we fail to do justice to their meaning throughout history, for surely they meant something to their original audience, and continue to speak to God's people today. Can we read them in a way that is faithful to their historical context and yet still relevant for us in our own time and place?

More than two thousand years have passed since the book of Daniel was written and reached its final form, and of course much has changed in that time. Yet much remains the same. No king named Nebuchadnezzar or Belshazzar reigns, and the Babylonian and Persian empires are long gone. Yet the wealthy and the powerful still seek to rule the world, and God's people still must decide which sovereign they truly serve. To whom do we owe our deepest allegiance, and how do we balance our obligations to God with our responsibilities as citizens? To whom do the kingdom, the power, and the glory belong? Are the kingdoms of this world and God's realm separate but equal realities, and is it possible to serve both God and the king?

Who Is Daniel?

What first attracted us to the book of Daniel was the mysterious figure of Daniel himself. Who is this Israelite noble swept up in the Babylonian exile, this youth favored by God, this interpreter of dreams and wise adviser to kings? What kind of man can pass God's judgment on rulers, survive being thrown into the lions' den, see visions of strange beasts and the Ancient of Days enthroned in splendor, and still remain humble, faithful, and constant in prayer? Why does the Daniel who can interpret and explain the visions of others in the first half of the book need help interpreting his own in the second half? What is the connection between the larger-than-life character we meet in the book and historical reality?

Several years ago we were invited to lead a series of Bible studies about Daniel for clergy colleagues. The more we read in preparation for the studies, the more Daniel intrigued us as a character and the more we wanted to discover the relationship between that character and the historical author or authors of the book that bears his name. Was Daniel a historical person? A fictional character? A cipher or symbol for some person or group? Caught up in the mystery of this individual and captivated by the message of the book that tells his story, we set out on a quest to find the real Daniel, wherever he might be hidden.

Daniel's identity might seem obvious at first—after all, in the last half of the book Daniel tells his own story in the first person. The first chapter of Daniel describes how he and his three friends came to live in King Nebuchadnezzar's court in Babylon, and the rest of the book is about Daniel's interactions with Nebuchadnezzar and his successors. At first glance, then, it appears that the book of Daniel was written by Daniel himself during the Babylonian exile.

But there are some problems with this apparently obvious answer. In the first place, the book of Daniel describes historical events that had not yet taken place during the Babylonian exile. For example, it gives an overview of the succession of empires that followed the Babylonians (including the empires of Alexander the Great and his successors), and the last half of the book demonstrates a detailed knowledge of the history of Antiochus IV Epiphanes and the early days of the Maccabean revolt, all characters and happenings dating to some four centuries *after* Nebuchadnezzar's reign. Some have argued that Daniel simply had the gift of prophecy and therefore could write history in advance. But if that is true, why is the book least accurate when it tells us about the Babylonian and Persian courts, the very context in which its hero is said to live? For example, it identifies Belshazzar as a king and as Nebuchadnezzar's son (Daniel 5:1–2), but in fact Belshazzar was the son of the Babylonian king, Nabonidus, and he served as regent but never as king. Daniel contains a number of errors of this sort regarding characters and events in the Babylonian and Persian periods. By contrast, the more closely the description of history approaches the Maccabean revolt, the more precise it becomes. Why would Daniel know more about the political situation four centuries after he died than he did about kings and historical occurrences during his own lifetime?

Complicating our quest to understand the mysterious figure of Daniel was the fact that not all Bibles contain the same version of the book. The version of Daniel found in Jewish and Protestant Bibles is translated from an original Hebrew and Aramaic text and is just twelve chapters long, while that of Roman Catholic and Orthodox Bibles, on the other hand, is based on a Greek version of Daniel and includes several additional chapters. The Septuagint—the earliest and most well known Greek version of the Hebrew Bible—was used by the first Christians and formed the basis for the Latin Vulgate, which became the official Bible of the Roman Catholic Church. To summarize the situation, Protestants and Jews read a shorter form of Daniel than Roman Catholics and Orthodox Christians do.

So what is in the longer Daniel, and where can this longer form be found? To answer the second question first, the additions to Daniel are printed with the Apocrypha in some study editions of Bibles. "The Prayer of Azariah" and the "Song of the Three Young Men" are inserted between Daniel 3:23 and 3:24, just after Hananiah, Mishael, and Azariah (more commonly known by their Babylonian names: Shadrach, Meshach, and Abednego) are thrown into the fiery furnace. Furthermore, Episcopalians may recognize the "Song of the Three Young Men" as the source of Canticles 12 ("A Song of Creation") and 13 ("A Song of Praise") in the Book of Common Prayer. Besides these prayers, the longer form of Daniel also includes two extra chapters that appear to be Greek versions of earlier Hebrew stories. Chapter 13 is printed in the Apocrypha as "Susanna," and tells the story of a virtuous woman who overcomes a false accusation of adultery with the help of Daniel's wisdom. Chapter 14, also known as "Bel and the Dragon," contains a story about the prophet Habakkuk delivering food to Daniel while he is in the lions' den as well as two humorous tales in which Daniel shows the foolishness of worshipping idols. In the first of these tales, Daniel cleverly exposes the tricks that the Babylonian priests use to create the illusion that their god Bel is alive; in the second he tells the king that without using a sword or club he will kill the great dragon that the Babylonians worship. Then he feeds cakes made out of pitch, fat, and hair to the dragon until it bursts open.

The colorful incidents described in "Susanna" and in "Bel and the Dragon" read more like fiction than like history. So do the entertaining stories in the first six chapters of Daniel, packed as they are with suspense and surprise. Who, then, was the true Daniel? Was he merely a fictional character in stories told to strengthen faith?

The earliest information that we have comes from the prophet Ezekiel, who wrote from exile in Babylon between 593 and 571 BCE. Since the first incidents in the book of Daniel take place during that same historical setting, we might naturally assume that Ezekiel and Daniel lived in the same place at roughly the same time. Ezekiel does not refer to Daniel as if he were a contemporary living with him in Babylon, however. Instead, he mentions Daniel together with Noah and Job as a model of righteousness: "Even if Noah, Daniel, and Job, these three, were in it [a land that sins against God], they would save only their own lives by their righteousness" (Ezekiel 14:14). It seems that by Ezekiel's time the historical Daniel was a figure lost in the mists of ancient history and obscured by legends.

In some ways what we learned about Daniel reminded us of other wise characters from Israel's past, such as Joseph, the interpreter of dreams in Genesis, and Methuselah's father Enoch (Genesis 5:18–24), who walked with God and then was no more, only to appear centuries later in the book of Enoch as a visionary who saw strange animals and caught glimpses of the heavenly court. This evidence suggests that like Enoch, Daniel was a familiar figure long before he appeared as a character in the book. Ezekiel shows us that tales about a wise man named Daniel already existed by the time that the Jews were exiled to Babylon in the sixth century BCE. Jews living after Ezekiel's time continued to recount the deeds of the wise and righteous Daniel, but they associated him with what was for them a more recent context—the royal court in Babylon. Some of those stories are preserved in Susanna and in Bel and the Dragon. Fragments of previously unknown tales about Daniel and the three young men have also been found among the Dead Sea Scrolls, so it seems clear that stories about Daniel were passed down by word of mouth over a period of centuries. Some of these narratives made their way into the Bible, and some did not. Thus the first six chapters of Daniel contain legends that predate the book itself.

The answers to our initial questions intensified our curiosity about the book of Daniel. If people already knew about Daniel, if stories about him were already circulating in the culture, why was the book written? Why does it highlight so forcefully Daniel's humility and his faithfulness to God, and not merely his extraordinary ability to interpret dreams and his wisdom? Why is it such an unusual combination of hero stories and bizarre visions?

The first six chapters of Daniel, with their descriptions of Daniel's dream interpretation and his rise to prominence in the king's court, are called "court tales," a genre of ancient literature that featured entertaining stories about the careers of people living in the royal court. Like modern-day historical fiction, this kind of story about the intrigues, rivalries, and ambitions of courtiers often combined facts about historically recognizable characters with novelistic details. It was well-known and popular not only in Israel but also among neighboring nations, especially Egypt, where most of the Joseph stories in Genesis take place. Like the stories of Joseph in Pharaoh's court or of Esther in the court of King Ahasuerus, the court tales in Daniel depict wise Jews finding a way to be faithful to God while surrounded by the temptations, luxuries, and conflicting loyalties of the royal lifestyle. Such tales were one form of wisdom literature, along with other forms such as the proverbs, riddles, and edifying lectures that we find in wisdom books like Proverbs, Ecclesiastes, and Job.

"Court tales" are a genre of ancient literature that featured entertaining stories about the careers, intrigues, and rivalries of people living in the royal court.

Wisdom literature addresses the question, "What does it mean to live a wise life?" and the answers can be surprisingly pragmatic. Proverbs, for example, includes advice about how to get ahead in the royal court and how to avoid unnecessary trouble, while the author of Ecclesiastes concludes, "This is what I have seen to be good: it is fitting to eat and drink and find enjoyment in all the toil with which one toils under the sun the few days of the life God gives us; for this is our lot" (Ecclesiastes 5:18).

If Daniel is wisdom literature, its heroes sometimes behave in unwise ways, at least according to conventional definitions of wisdom. Proverbs outlines wise behavior for the courtier: "My child, fear the LORD and the king, and do not disobey either of them" (Proverbs 24:21). Again it advises, "A king's wrath is a messenger of death, and whoever is wise will appease it" (Proverbs 16:14). As Daniel and friends discover, such advice may sound good in theory, but putting it into practice is not always easy. When God's laws and the king's edicts directly contradict each other—as when the king commands all his subjects to bow down to a golden statue—how can they obey both God and the king? In such situations Daniel and his friends do not always act like the prudent courtier who does his best to avoid upsetting the king. At times they flatly disobey the king's orders or pronounce judgment on his actions, acting more like prophets speaking truth to power than like typical wise men. Their behavior invites us to consider the question: what does it mean to be wise when the king's will and God's will stand in conflict with each other?

Being wise is often defined as being educated. The truly wise person, however, perceives life as a gift and has an exceptional capacity to grasp its meaning. Scholars have book learning; the wise know the boundaries between life and death. Scholars know how to do research and dedicate themselves to acquiring valuable knowledge, preserving it, and passing it on. The wise, on the other hand, explore the limits of the human condition and develop a deep understanding of human conduct and human nature. Scholars are shaped by their scholarly disciplines and their own hard work, but the wise attribute their vision of life to powers greater than themselves.

The book of Daniel brings scholarship and wisdom together in a single character. Daniel is the legendary wise man from the past, but he is also a scholar and courtier who has much in common with the scribes. The stories in the first six chapters link the legendary Daniel of old with the scribes and sages who since ancient times had studied the scriptures and the stars, interpreting the present, discerning the outline of the future and, sometimes, presenting events that had already taken place as if they were predictions of what was still to come.

In biblical times only the elite knew how to read and write. Among that elite were the scribes, who were the people in charge of keeping and consulting the historical records and writing down laws and various kinds of legal documents. They lived in the royal courts and the palaces of the nobility, and in their capacity as advisors to nobles and kings they had to cultivate the ability to speak the truth with great discretion. Israel's scribes were also entrusted with preserving oral traditions, studying traditional literature, and copying and interpreting the scriptures. They earned their living by working for kings and nobles, but because they were students of the scriptures, they also served as interpreters of God's word for the common people of Israel. At times their multiple roles placed them in nearly impossible situations. For example, Jeremiah—a member of the priestly nobility as well as a prophet—commanded his scribe Baruch to write down his prophetic message and read it to all the people in the temple as a way of calling them to repentance. When Baruch read Jeremiah's words in the temple, King Jehoiakim caught wind of it, cut up and burned the scroll, and ordered that both Baruch and Jeremiah be arrested (Jeremiah 36:4–32). Difficult political situations like Baruch's meant that the scribes had to be carefully trained in the ways of the world and the realities of court life. Wisdom literature, which often focuses on such topics, is the type of biblical literature most often associated with the scribes.

Although the first part of Daniel is typically understood as wisdom literature, the last half is not. Like the Joseph stories, the stories in Daniel 1–6 are written in the third person. At the beginning of chapter 7, however, the style of writing abruptly changes as Daniel begins to speak in the first person. Chapters 7 through12, which contain his descriptions of encounters with angelic beings and visions of scenes in heaven, look more like the book of Revelation than like the book of Proverbs. This last half of the book is usually regarded as apocalyptic literature.

The term "apocalyptic" means "uncovering." Apocalyptic literature is the literature of revelation. It is a genre characterized by bizarre visions, mysterious glimpses of the divine court, strange encounters with heavenly messengers, and epic battles between the forces of good and the forces of evil. Aided by the divine messenger, the seer who describes the visions interprets their significance for the readers and discloses God's plan for history. Most apocalyptic literature was written during times of great persecution and danger for God's people.

Apocalyptic is the literature of revelation, characterized by bizarre visions, mysterious glimpses of the divine court, encounters with heavenly messengers, and epic battles between good and evil.

At first glance apocalyptic literature may seem to be about the end of the world, and indeed many interpreters read it as if it were. But apocalyptic books like Daniel and Revelation pay attention to whole historical eras rather than focusing merely on the end of history. They describe the behavior of earthly rulers and the devastating impact that their economic and religious decisions have on their subjects. They especially emphasize the overwhelming violence and destruction that kings inflict in their campaigns to conquer new territories and maintain power over their kingdoms. Sometimes, because their current situation looks so bleak, the authors of apocalyptic books find it necessary to assure their readers that this present age is not the final word and the eternal God is at work to bring hope beyond history. For the most part, however, the authors of apocalyptic books are focused on a point long before the end of the world. They are writing about the end of empires.

Nevertheless, apocalyptic literature offers more than a message of judgment on empires. It also helps us to imagine a different kind of domain and another way of living that stands in stark contrast to the brutality of tyrants. It paints pictures of peaceful rulers who seek the well-being not only of their own people but of all nations. Apocalyptic literature envisions another possible world, a just society that begins whenever and wherever God's people live into God's dream for the world.

Apocalyptic literature offers more than a message of judgment on empires. It also helps us to imagine a different kind of domain and another way of living that stands in stark contrast to the brutality of tyrants.

It is in the apocalyptic section of Daniel that we see the fingerprints of the book's authors most clearly. The scribes who wrote down the legends about Daniel's wise dealings with emperors combined this traditional material with new stories about Daniel's visions of the time when Israel's conquerors would be overthrown. By the time that they wrote the book, the Babylonians and the Persians were ancient history as far as the people of Israel were concerned. Although the book of Daniel tells about his dealings with Babylonian and Persian kings, its original readers would have recognized many details, especially in the apocalyptic parts of the book, that described the events of their own time. When a group of scribes composed the book of Daniel, God's faithful people were facing a new set of challenges: life under the rule of Antiochus IV Epiphanes.

The History behind Daniel

Time after time the book of Daniel depicts the clash between its heroes' faith and the religion of the king. It portrays the challenges and temptations that Daniel and his friends face as they adapt to life in the imperial court. In order to understand the situation of the characters and the message of the book, readers need to know a little Israelite history.

From the beginning the people of Israel and Judah were threatened by superpowers such as Egypt, Assyria, and Babylon. Nevertheless, for a period of more than four hundred years, Abraham's descendants enjoyed some form of independence in Canaan under their own kings. David and his son Solomon reigned over the entire region from the Sea of Galilee to the wilderness west of the Dead Sea, but after Solomon's death the realm divided into two kingdoms, Israel in the north and Judah in the south. In 722–721 BCE, roughly two hundred years after that division, the Assyrians conquered Israel and exiled many of its people. The southern kingdom of Judah survived the fall of Israel, however, and David's descendants continued to reign over Judah until the early sixth century.

In 587–586 BCE King Nebuchadnezzar of Babylon conquered Judah and destroyed Jerusalem, including the temple that Solomon had built there for Yahweh. Over the course of a decade, he exiled the nobility and the bulk of the Jewish population to Babylonia, in the part of the world that is now known as Iraq. Nebuchadnezzar's empire extended from the Persian Gulf to the border of Egypt, and

Babylon was its capital city. The psalmist poignantly evokes the desolation of the Jews during this period in their history:

By the rivers of Babylon—
there we sat down and there we wept
when we remembered Zion.
On the willows there
we hung up our harps.
For there our captors
asked us for songs,
and our tormentors asked for mirth, saying,
"Sing us one of the songs of Zion!"
How could we sing the LORD's song
in a foreign land? (Psalm 137:1–4)

Thus the people of Judah confronted daunting challenges in Babylon. They arrived destitute and in shock, having seen friends, relatives, and even their own children slaughtered before their eyes. They had to find some way to survive in this foreign land by learning a new language and adapting to new customs, new foods, and a whole new culture. Furthermore, their religion had centered around animal sacrifice, which had been permitted only in the temple in Jerusalem. Now they were so far from their homeland that even if the temple had still existed, they would have had to find a way to worship without it.

For more than a generation, the people of Judah lived in exile under Babylonian rule. Then a new world power arose on the scene. Cyrus the Great of Persia conquered Babylon in 539 BCE. As a general policy, he returned the exiles captured by the Babylonians to their native countries and rebuilt the temples that the Babylonians had destroyed. Many Jews returned to their homeland at this time, rebuilt Jerusalem and the temple, and worked to reestablish themselves as a community and restore their religious identity. Not everyone, however, went home to the land of Israel. Some Jews chose to stay in Babylon and adapt to life under Persian rule.

Even the Jews who returned to their ancestral homeland were not free of foreign domination. For the next four centuries, Israel continued to be controlled by a succession of rulers. After the Persians came

Alexander the Great. When Alexander died, his empire was divided among his generals, and the next several centuries saw the Ptolemaic and Seleucid dynasties they founded fighting for control over Israel and the other nations that inhabited the narrow strip of fertile land between Egypt and Mesopotamia.

The power wielded by this succession of dynasties was not simply a matter of political control or of heavy taxation. It extended into everyday life because it included direct efforts to change the cultures of the conquered peoples. Already during the Babylonian and Persian periods the exiles had experienced the pressure to assimilate, to give up their distinctive cultural and religious practices in an effort to blend more seamlessly into the larger society. From Alexander's time on, however, this pressure intensified tremendously. Alexander, who had been tutored by the Greek philosopher Aristotle, was dedicated to propagating Greek culture. He developed highly effective tactics for spreading the Greek way of life, such as promoting the Greek language as the official language of politics and trade. He advocated religious syncretism, arguing, for example, that Venus, Aphrodite, and Ishtar were really all the same goddess worshipped under different names, and that Zeus, Jupiter, and Yahweh were all the same god. Furthermore, he established Greek-style cities wherever he went, settling them with his own soldiers and making them the community centers for outlying areas. The cultural institutions common to these Greek cities created special challenges for Jews.

For example, public sacrifices to pagan deities were an essential part of every civic occasion, and anyone who refused to participate was not only blasphemous but politically suspect, since religion was an inseparable part of the state's power. Another particularly difficult aspect of Greek culture was the gymnasium. As the centerpiece of the Greek educational system, it was a vital part of any Greek colony, where young men studied grammar, rhetoric, and philosophy. During the centuries after Alexander, education in the gymnasium was a prerequisite for success in the world. But because

> The cultural institutions of Greek cities created special challenges for Jews. Public sacrifices to pagan deities were an essential part of every civic occasion, and anyone who refused to participate was not only blasphemous but politically suspect.

young men in the gymnasium honed both their minds and their bodies, exercising in the nude, this was problematic for Jewish males. (In fact, the word "gymnasium" is derived from the Greek word *gymnos,* or "naked.") In this environment they were easily identifiable. Circumcision was the sign that marked them as belonging to God's chosen people, the children of Abraham, while not belonging to the broader culture. Their circumcisions set them apart as different, even strange, in a culture where anyone who wanted to get ahead was trying to blend into the Greek ideal.

In the early second century, the pressure for Jews to assimilate to the dominant Greek culture became stronger and more explicit. By this period the historic homeland of the Jews was controlled by the Syrian Seleucid dynasty. In 169 BCE the arrogant and brutal Seleucid King Antiochus IV entered the temple in Jerusalem, stripped it of its gold and silver furnishings, and carried away all its valuable contents to Syria. Two years later Antiochus returned from a humiliating defeat in Egypt determined to demonstrate that despite this military failure, he was still a powerful ruler. He attacked Jerusalem, killing many people and burning parts of the city. His subsequent actions were a frontal assault on the Jewish religion—under his new policy, anyone who prayed to Yahweh, observed the Sabbath, circumcised a child, or owned a copy of the Jewish scriptures received the death penalty. Striking at the very heart of the Jewish faith, moreover, Antiochus built an altar to Zeus directly over the altar of burnt offering in the Jerusalem temple and sacrificed a pig—an unclean animal—to Zeus there. He even claimed the title Epiphanes, "God Manifest," identifying himself as divine and therefore worthy of worship. Then he put in place a system of inspectors to enforce the new laws and to punish the Jews by torture and death if they failed to obey.

The books of 1 and 2 Maccabees vividly record the Jews' response to Antiochus' act of blasphemy. When one of Antiochus' agents commanded the people in the town of Modein to offer sacrifice in violation of Jewish law, a priest named Mattathias killed the officer, tore down the altar, and called the people of Judah and Jerusalem to rise up in revolt. Led by his sons Judas Maccabeus, Jonathan, and Simon, the Jews fought a series of battles against Antiochus' army. In 164, after three years of war, the rebels recaptured Jerusalem. They repaired, purified, and rededicated the temple, an event now celebrated in the feast of Hanukah. Over time the Hasmonean dynasty founded by Mattathias' sons consolidated the Jewish drive toward independence, while in a move that angered many who argued for strict observance of Jewish law, Jonathan and some of his successors also served as high priests. The Jewish state established by the Hasmoneans enjoyed independence until the Roman general Pompey entered Jerusalem in 63 BCE.

The Figure of Daniel

The figure of Daniel himself reflects the challenges and the difficulties that the scribes and people were facing throughout this history. He seeks to remain faithful to the Sovereign God, and in the process he learns the necessity of humility, of prayer, of confession, of risking everything as he stands up to the merciless earthly powers. He does all these things because he knows that he owes everything he is and everything he has to the grace and mercy of God. Daniel is wise and absolutely loyal to God. Yet when he sees incomprehensible visions and terrifying beasts, he personifies the limitations that every human being faces. He symbolizes courage and the search for God, but in his moments of weakness and pride he also reflects the selfish ambitions that weaken and impoverish human beings. In story after story he communicates the message that human beings will never reach their goals if they try to achieve everything on their own terms, independently from the one God. Ultimately God alone controls the outcome of human dreams.

As a character, the faithful Daniel is not a single historical person, although the book's depiction of the struggle to remain faithful to God as the true sovereign reflects real historical situations. Laughable and exaggerated litanies of characters and instruments—"the magicians, the enchanters, the sorcerers, and the Chaldeans" (2:2); "the satraps, the prefects, and the governors, the counselors, the treasurers, the justices, the magistrates, and all the officials of the provinces" (3:2); "the horn, pipe, lyre, trigon, harp, drum, and entire musical ensemble" (3:5)—what are these but signs of a confrontation between a culture that recognizes only one God and the cultures of conquerors who worship many gods and deify mortal rulers? The Daniel whom we find in the midst of that confrontation has grown into something much more than the historical person who lies behind the legends. He represents the authors of the book that bears his name, a group of scribes and prophets who dedicated themselves to affirming that the God of heaven is the only God, true and sovereign, in direct confrontation with the political powers of this world. Furthermore, he brings together in a single figure the struggles of the Jewish people from the time of their exile in Babylon, through their life under Persian rule, on into the age of Alexander the Great and, eventually Antiochus IV.

During the Maccabean revolt, a group of scribes collected the legends about Daniel that seemed most relevant to the current historical situation. Stories about heroes who chose to be thrown into the fiery furnace rather than worship a golden idol, or to be cast into the lions' den rather than give up their daily prayers, must have spoken powerfully to ordinary Jews living under Antiochus' tyrannical reign. Along with these dramatic tales, the scribes included subtler traditional material that spoke to the challenges and temptations they themselves faced in their daily dealings with the nobility—how Daniel and his friends refused to be won over by the luxuries of the imperial court, for example, or how Daniel navigated the politics of the court and managed the royal ego. The scribes arranged and revised these stories, and then composed additional materials to make the book's message even more relevant for the crisis that the people of God were facing under the rule of Antiochus IV Epiphanes. The apocalyptic visions at the end of the book encouraged a persecuted people to believe that God was still involved with their history and that the brutal king would not have the last word.

To sum up the situation, the book of Daniel plants its roots in the Babylonian exile, while its final form is descriptive of the situation just before the end of the Maccabean revolt. The hero stories at the beginning of the book are designed to help us to interpret the apocalyptic portions, and the apocalyptic chapters provide a larger and more analytic context for the hero stories. Together, they confront us with a pressing question: how can God's people remain faithful while living in a world dominated by rulers and systems that oppose God?

Knowing that the book of Daniel was written during the Maccabean revolt helps us to:

- understand Daniel's message as a courageous call to obey God in an era when it would have been far safer and more politic to obey the king;
- take into account that, by combining traditional stories with later materials, Daniel portrays the subtle pressures to conform to the dominant society as well as the more violent consequences of refusal to obey the powers that be;
- explore Daniel's strategy of nonviolent resistance as a deliberate alternative to approaches taken by other groups at the time; and
- recognize the parallels between Daniel's situation and the challenges that Christians around the world face today.

Our conclusion that the book of Daniel was written by a group of scribes during the Maccabean period rather than by an actual person named Daniel during the Babylonian exile means, of course, that the book was written under a pseudonym. Today we might consider pseudonymous writing as deceitful and dishonest, but would it be fair to call Daniel a forgery? Were the first readers of Daniel being deceived by its authors?

Daniel confronts us with a pressing question: how can God's people remain faithful while living in a world dominated by rulers and systems that oppose God?

As we have discussed above, Daniel is a blending of genres, part court tale, part wisdom literature, and part apocalyptic. Both court tales and apocalyptic literature were often associated with well-known heroes. The heroes in apocalyptic literature were typically great figures of the distant past such as Enoch, Adam, or Moses. In many apocalyptic books such heroes give first-person descriptions of visions that they have received or experiences that have been interpreted for them by divine messengers. Because such figures were from so far back in time, often from a thousand years or more before the books about them were written, the first readers of apocalyptic works such as the *Assumption of Moses* understood the first-person vision reports in these books as a literary device rather than as straightforward historical reporting. Much like the later editors who added the heading "of

David" to many psalms to honor Israel's musician-king by continuing his musical tradition, authors of pseudonymous apocalyptic works perceived themselves as honoring the authority in whose name they wrote and as continuing in the same sacred tradition of interpretation. The first-person narration in Daniel fits into the same kind of category.

Surely the readers of Daniel knew, when the book first appeared on the scene, that it had not been written by Daniel. They were already familiar with court tales about Daniel, and they knew that he had lived many centuries before their time. The vision reports in this new book were consistent with the themes running through those traditional stories, however, and Daniel was an appropriate character to be the medium for the apocalyptic message tailored for the readers' own day: "Remain faithful to God, take courage, and obey God despite the consequences. No matter what happens at this moment in history, God is still on the throne."

If we look at the contents of the Bible even briefly, it soon becomes apparent that God is not limited to a single way of communicating with us. The Bible contains historical books, it is true, but it is also rich with parables, poetry, wisdom sayings, songs, letters, and even humor. Consider the teachings of Jesus, for example. His stories about the Good Samaritan and about the Prodigal Son are fictional, and yet they communicate profound truths about the nature of God's love for us. His parables of the Two Sons (Matthew 21:28–32) and the Wicked Tenants (Matthew 21:33–45) are fictional, and yet they also incorporate historical facts to teach about the way that God works in history. Jesus' parables demonstrate that narratives can combine fiction and fact in the service of God's truth.

In his commentary on Daniel, scholar Choon-Leong Seow compares Daniel to works of art such as Shakespeare's *Julius Caesar* and Leonardo da Vinci's *Last Supper*. Both of these compositions deal with historical events, and both contain anachronisms or errors of fact; both are considered masterpieces. Their value does not depend on the artists' mastery of historical detail, but on their insight into the larger truths of human nature and of history. Seow concludes, "So, too, the value of the book of Daniel as scripture does not depend on the historical accuracy of the props on its literary stage, but on the power of its theological message. The authority of the book as scripture lies in its power to inspire and shape the community of faith."[4] The book of Daniel was accepted as Scripture because, as God's people read it over the course of centuries and in many different contexts, they heard God's word speaking to them with grace and power.

Ways of Reading Daniel

The book of Daniel has been influential throughout Christian history. Its ideas and terminology were adapted for reuse in the New Testament, and over the centuries since the New Testament era, many different interpreters have offered their readings of Daniel's message. The interest in Daniel has continued into our own day. Many contemporary interpreters of Daniel treat the book in one of the following ways:

- as a coded prediction of events in our own time;
- as an historical puzzle in need of a solution;
- as a call to inaction; or
- as resistance literature.

But do any of these ways of approaching Daniel do it justice?

Some of the most widely read interpretations of Daniel, including those on which the best-selling *Left Behind* series depends, see the book as a series of predictions about people, organizations, and situations in the modern world. Most recently, Harold Camping used the 2,300 days mentioned in Daniel 8:14 as a key element in the calculations that led to his failed prediction that Christ would return on May 21, 2011. Similarly, Hal Lindsey, whose influential bestseller *The Late Great Planet Earth* set off a wave of end-time speculation when it was published in 1970, argues that Daniel predicts the revival of the Roman Empire in our era. Lindsey even identifies the European Common Market as the ten-horned beast described in Daniel 7. Camping, Lindsey, and other interpreters like them read the imagery in Daniel in light of imagery from the book of Revelation, from the gospels, and from Paul's letters without paying attention to the historical contexts and integrity of the individual books. This way of reading ignores what we have learned from ancient literature, coins, and artifacts about the probable original meaning of symbols such as the statue made of many different metals in Daniel, or the number 666 in Revelation. Furthermore, it seems to presuppose that Daniel was meaningless to its original readers. If the book is merely an elaborate secret message that, once decoded, identifies organizations such as the United Nations as the work of the devil, why was it read and valued by Jews and Christians during the more than two thousand years between its composition and our own time? Did God have no word to speak through Daniel to Jews living under Antiochus IV's persecution, to Christians suffering under the Romans, or to all those in every age who have sought to obey God no matter what the cost? Out of all the generations who have lived and died since the book was written, do we alone matter to God? Reading Daniel with so little regard for history not only fails the test of scholarly credibility; it is an affront to the character of a loving God who speaks to the faithful in every age.

If Daniel is merely an elaborate secret message to be decoded, then why was it read and valued by Jews and Christians during the more than two thousand years between its composition and our own time?

While the *Left Behind* style of reading may be accused of ignoring history, some commentators go to the other extreme and focus on historical detail to the virtual exclusion of other concerns. They treat Daniel as little more than a historical puzzle, and they have very little to say about its theological emphases except as an example of the views of a particular faction within the Judaism of the day. Although such research is an invaluable resource for biblical scholars, it is of limited value for anyone who seeks to apply the Bible's message to our lives today. In this book, we will use the results of careful historical research to offer an interpretation of Daniel that respects both its historical context and its authority as a book through which God continues to speak to us now.

Two other common approaches to Daniel take the book's historical context seriously, but understand its response to that context in contradictory ways. Both approaches focus on the book's setting within the Maccabean period, when Judas Maccabeus and his brothers were leading the Jewish people in an armed revolt against Antiochus IV Epiphanes. One group of commentators perceives Daniel largely as a reaction against the Maccabean revolt, arguing that the court stories in Daniel advocate a passive approach, thus teaching by example that Jews should adapt to the king's demands and learn to live within the system instead of revolting against it. According to these interpreters, since there is nothing that God's people can do to change the situation themselves, they must simply wait for God to act. The other group understands Daniel as resistance literature designed to encourage the faithful to stand firm in their armed political struggles against their Syrian rulers. This group places more emphasis on the last half of Daniel and points to passages such as Daniel 11:29–35 as evidence that the author viewed the Maccabean revolt favorably, even if it offered only "a little help."

Our own understanding of the book differs from all of the preceding approaches. While we agree with those who contend that the book was composed in its final form just before or during the Maccabean revolt, we also take seriously its inclusion of traditions that date to a much earlier time. Daniel reflects a centuries-long history of coping with empire in its many and varied forms. Our interpretation seeks to read the book as a whole, with attention to each of its component parts. As a result, we see the book as speaking not only to those who are confronting violent political oppression, but also to those who face the more subtle pressure to placate the rich and the powerful in order to get ahead in the world. The heroes in Daniel model both nonviolent resistance to evil and faithfulness amid the temptations of the royal court. Through stories, visions, and dreams, the book of Daniel calls all its readers to confess not only with their lips, but with their lives, that God alone is sovereign over every earthly power.

Daniel's call to faithful living still resonates in the twenty-first century. Although the political shape of empire has changed greatly in the more than two millennia since Daniel was written, a few powerful nations still exert tremendous influence over the lives and destinies of millions who live outside their boundaries. In addition, a new kind of empire—a global economy dominated by multinational corporations—brings wealth to some corners of the world at the same time that it devastates others. The aggressive marketing of soft drinks and similar products extends even to the most impoverished pockets of the globe, while long-cherished local customs, traditions, and languages disappear in the rush to conform to an increasingly homogeneous global culture. In many ways, those closest to the centers of power are the last to perceive what is happening because they seldom see the impact that their choices have on people in other parts of the world. Is this a new phenomenon? Yes. But in many ways it resembles an old one.

Like us, Daniel's original audience lived under the influence of economic and political forces that transformed culture across the known world and threatened to annihilate local ways of life. The book of Daniel treats this situation not simply as a matter of economics or politics, but as a question of faith. At the very heart of Daniel's message lies the claim that God alone is sovereign, and that the kingdoms of this world are subject to God. For the authors of Daniel, political violence, greed, extravagance, and the domination of the defenseless are not simply political problems. They are religious issues because they are intimately bound up with the question of what it means to be fully human. The sovereign God calls the privileged and the powerful to use their wealth and power for the well-being of all people. As Nebuchadnezzar ultimately confesses, "all [God's] works are truth, and his ways are justice; and he is able to bring low those who walk in pride" (4:37).

> For the authors of Daniel, political violence, greed, extravagance, and the domination of the defenseless are not simply political problems, but religious issues intimately bound up with the question of what it means to be fully human.

The human hunger for self-glorification stands in contrast to the confession of God as creator and sovereign. For Daniel, worshipping golden statues is only the most obvious form of idolatry. The book invites its readers to see that images imprinted in the mind may be as dangerous as images graven in stone, and that the interpretation of images may lead either to healthy or to distorted understandings of God, the self, and the world. For example, when Daniel interprets Nebuchadnezzar's dream, the self-image that Nebuchadnezzar cherishes in his own heart and mind prompts the king to reinterpret Daniel's words and ultimately leads him to fashion an idol to which others must bow down. So also in our day it may be instructive to consider how the seductive power of images and their exploitation by the media and by commercial interests lead people to imagine their own empowerment as the greatest good and the fulfillment of their desires as the most essential need.

In stark contrast to such a worldview, Daniel invites its readers to learn the humility that flows from a life of prayer. The regular practice of prayer and worship allows Daniel to honor God as the giver and to recognize himself as the recipient of God's power and grace. Thus the humility that Daniel models and teaches is not groveling or self-abasement, but rather a confession of God as the source of all that is. True confession of the one God leads to a right confession of human worth. For Daniel, humans are God's beloved, created in God's likeness, and by God's power called to be transformed more and more into the image of God.

The divine call for humanity's transformation is one aspect of a larger divine purpose for the creation. In hymns, dreams, and visions, Daniel criticizes the world as it is and portrays the world as God intends it to be. The new reality envisioned is not utopia as the term has traditionally been understood; it is not the impossible dream of the naive and the powerless. Instead, Daniel shows its readers another possible world, a just society brought about by God's power at work among those who obey the call. Although the full flowering of that society awaits the end of days, the seed takes root and grows wherever people honor God's sovereignty and seek to live as members of God's domain. In the chapters that follow, we will explore the ways in which Daniel pronounces God's judgment on the world as it is, offers an alternative vision of God's desire for the creation, and invites its readers to participate in God's work of making that dream a reality.

Which Lord?

The book begins with a series of stories about Daniel and his friends Hananiah, Mishael, and Azariah, better known to most of us as Shadrach, Meshach, and Abednego. These young men's faithfulness to God is tested repeatedly as they face one challenge after another. In the first chapter they are selected for privileged positions in Nebuchadnezzar's court and offered delicacies from the king's table, while in the second, Daniel interprets Nebuchadnezzar's dream about a strange statue with a golden head and clay feet. The third tells the familiar tale of the three young men in the fiery furnace; the fourth, Nebuchadnezzar's dream about a great tree and the account of his madness; and the fifth, Belshazzar's feast and the handwriting on the wall. The series concludes with perhaps the most beloved story of all, which is Daniel in the lions' den. In one way or another, each of the first six chapters invites us to ask ourselves, Who is the true king? And which Lord do we really serve?

As we mentioned earlier, stories about these four young men appear outside the Bible, too. Why were these tales so popular, and why did the authors of Daniel choose to include them in their book? In the first part of this chapter, we will discuss the role that stories in general and these in particular play in shaping faith, forming character, and enabling us to see the connection between our lives and God's purpose for the world. Then we will focus on Daniel 1 and show how its tale of the young men's first days in the royal court helped its original readers to recognize the temptations that they encountered every day. The story confronts both them and us with several fundamental questions. Who is the source of our life and our hope? Which do we value more—safety, a comfortable life, and success? Or God? To whom, ultimately, do we owe our deepest allegiance?

Such questions are raised frequently in Scripture, and when they are stated so starkly, the answers may seem commonplace and rather obvious. The advantage of stories like those in Daniel is that they bring new depth both to the questions and to their answers by capturing our imaginations and helping us to visualize the complexities of serving God in the real world more fully than abstract statements ever could. At the same time, they show us a way to live faithfully and invite us to step onto the path ourselves.

Stories can motivate people and offer hope even in seemingly hopeless situations. And they have other advantages. Consider, for example, the role that the story of Moses and the Exodus has played in African-American culture. Slaves working in the field sang,

> When Israel was in Egypt's land
> Let my people go
> Oppress'd so hard they could not stand
> Let my people go.
> Go down, Moses,
> Way down to Egypt's land.
> Tell old Pharaoh,
> Let my people go.

They were describing their own enslavement, singing about their longing for freedom, but how could their masters object? It was just a biblical story. As the slaves toiled in the hot sun and suffered under the overseer's whip, the story of the Exodus helped them remember God's love and justice. It pronounced God's judgment on their masters and assured them that God is always on the side of freedom. It gave them hope that God would raise up a new Moses who would free God's people and lead them into the promised land. And it prepared them to follow that new Moses, whenever and wherever he might appear.

Generations later, when Martin Luther King Jr. rallied the descendants of the slaves and called them to protest nonviolently until they were granted their civil rights, he turned again to the Exodus, placing himself in the pivotal role of Moses. But on the night before he was assassinated, King focused on a different part of the story. By this time, he suggested, God's people had left Egypt. They had been freed from slavery but had not yet reached the land flowing with milk and honey. With the help of God, he had led them on the long journey toward that land, but now it looked as if it might be time for new leadership. So King compared himself to Moses, who died in the wilderness just after God allowed him to climb Mount Nebo and see the land of Canaan from afar. "I've been to the mountaintop," King said. "And I've looked over. And I've seen the Promised Land. I may not get there with you. But I want you to know tonight, that we, as a people, will get to the Promised Land." Through the old, familiar story King energized the crowd and gave them not just an abstract promise, but a vision. They became the Israelites, journeying through the wilderness, sometimes weary and hungry and frightened, but never alone. They could picture the land flowing with milk and honey, and imagine Joshua rising up to lead them after Moses' death. The biblical story came alive once more, giving shape to the hopes of a new generation.

Like the story of the Exodus in African-American culture, the tales about Daniel and his friends helped God's captive people to imagine freedom. They gave the Jews a way to remind each other of God's justice and God's promises covertly, defying their masters even as they suffered under their tyranny. They helped them to see what faithfulness might look like and how God could be at work even in seemingly impossible situations. Furthermore, because they dealt so explicitly with the challenges of life under foreign rule, they enabled the Jews to maintain their identity as God's

The tales about Daniel and his friends helped God's captive people to imagine freedom, and gave the Jews a way to remind each other of God's justice and God's promises covertly, defying their masters even as they suffered under their tyranny.

people despite conquest, exile, and all the historical forces that might have prompted them to abandon both faith and hope.

The stories that eventually came to be collected in the book of Daniel were passed down orally in Israel from one generation to the next. They come from an evolving community that lived and defined itself through recounting past experiences. As a character in these narratives, Daniel is much like King Arthur or Robin Hood, a figure rooted in the distant past who has attained legendary status over time. A person named Dan-El was depicted in the ancient Canaanite legend of Aqhat as one who, because of his wisdom and virtue, was able to save his son from death. By the time of the Babylonian exile, when Ezekiel prophesied to the people of Judah, the legend of Dan-El had grown until Ezekiel could mention him in the same breath with Noah and Job as an exemplary figure, a paragon of righteousness and wisdom (Ezekiel 14:14, 20; 28:3). As a result, when Jews read the tale of Daniel and his friends in the court of Nebuchadnezzar, they would have known what kind of role Daniel would play there and in the narratives that followed. He is an idealized figure through whom the narrator shows the reader how to live wisely and faithfully even in the most difficult and dangerous situations.

As often happens with material that has been passed down by word of mouth, the stories in the first half of Daniel all have a similar structure. A king appears, together with his advisers; the hero or heroes must overcome a challenge; their lives hang in the balance; with the help of God, they successfully overcome all obstacles. This structural repetition makes the stories easier to remember and allows them to function collectively to reinforce several key theological points. Daniel's career in the court of the conquerors gave Jews a framework for thinking about the costs and consequences of serving God. What does a faithful life look like? What kinds of temptations had God's children faced before? What had they done to overcome temptation? How had God been involved in their lives?

The court stories in Daniel, like other memories passed down from one generation to the next, often have an elusive and imprecise quality. The basic outline of the story persists, but the details are not necessarily clear or consistent. To understand this better, think about stories that have been handed down within your own family—you know that these tales are based on actual occurrences, but you may not always be sure exactly when certain events happened, or even to whom. Over time, stories that were originally about Great Uncle Bob may be attributed to Great Uncle Arthur. But the details and the historical factuality of our family stories become less important than the narrative itself, because the stories tell us who our families are and who we are. They shape us and help to give our lives meaning.

The stories about Daniel and his friends became a tool for the people of Israel to talk not only about who these heroic young men were, but also about who they themselves were and who they wanted to be. Because the stories were told not just in one community but throughout the nation, they were enriched over time by other communities' reflections on their own experiences and the challenges that they faced as they sought to remain faithful to God even while they lived in a culture with values very different from their own. Eventually these tales from Daniel's life became the story not only of Daniel, but of a suffering people facing oppression, an entire nation that confronted forces opposed to their God. The storytellers knew from experience that choosing to obey the king might require them to compromise or even abandon their loyalty to God; on the other hand, choosing to obey God in spite of the king's commands might cost them their lives. Incorporating their own experiences into the stories gave the tales an ongoing life and helped God's people to hold on to hope in the midst of violence and destruction.

> *These tales from Daniel's life became the story not only of Daniel, but of a suffering people facing oppression, an entire nation that confronted forces opposed to their God.*

Daniel 1: Who Is in Charge?

As the book of Daniel begins, it appears that Nebuchadnezzar is in control of Judah's destiny, and the first verse is all about Nebuchadnezzar's attack on the city: "In the third year of the reign of King Jehoiakim of Judah, King Nebuchadnezzar of Babylon came to Jerusalem and besieged it." In the very next verse, however, the narrator focuses on what God does: "And my Lord gave Jehoiakim king of Judah into his hand, along with some of the vessels from the house of God. These he carried off to the house of his gods in the land of Shinar and put in the treasure house of his gods" (1:2, our translation). In these first verses the narrator actually attributes Nebuchadnezzar's victory to God's will: Nebuchadnezzar conquers Jehoiakim *only* because God wills it, and the sacred vessels from the Jerusalem temple reside in the temple of pagan gods only because God gives them into Nebuchadnezzar's hand.

Daniel's opening paragraph sets up the contrast between surface appearances and deeper reality that will be emphasized repeatedly throughout the book. Like a tap on the shoulder and a pointed finger, it prompts us to look past the obvious trappings of power in order to see who is really in control. Don't be deceived by appearances, the narrator seems to say. No matter how dire the present circumstances might be, the story is still unfolding. God's people can trust God to be faithful. It might look as if the present belongs to the king, but the end of the story belongs to God.

The first chapter of Daniel also sets up a choice that will confront the characters (and by extension, the readers) throughout the whole book: who is the true sovereign? Already the narrator has called God "my Lord" (1:2, in Hebrew, *Adonai*), thus making his own allegiance clear. Ashpenaz the palace master, on the other hand, serves Nebuchadnezzar, whom he calls "my lord [*adoni*] the king" (1:10). In the middle stand Daniel and the three young men. They are Israelites who worship the God of Israel, but they have been summoned to the palace to be trained for Nebuchadnezzar's court. And so the drama begins: which lord will they serve?

We should not underestimate the courage it would have taken to serve God in such a context. Nebuchadnezzar's power was all around them in their everyday experience of the world, in the sights and sounds and smells of ordinary life, for ancient kings celebrated their power through visual art and by recounting the stories of their conquests. The Assyrian king Sennacherib, for example, decorated his palace in Nineveh with reliefs showing his army torturing and impaling Judean soldiers, while the Babylonians and Persians erected monuments throughout their empires depicting their military triumphs and portraying the humiliation of their enemies in graphic detail. Religious festivals often included processions, songs, and stories that retold the victories of the rulers and reinforced the defeat of subject peoples who now served their conquerors. Living in the capital city, and especially living in the palace, would have meant being surrounded by constant reminders of Judah's subject status. The conquerors defined the terms and conditions by which the conquered lived. If history is a story told by the winners, how do the losers keep their identity and their religious faith from being distorted or lost altogether?

The narrator of Daniel does not deny the story told by the winners, yet the court tales in Daniel provide God's people with stories that they can claim as their own, tales in which the rulers are exposed as flawed, vulnerable, and accountable to a power greater than themselves. In the process, there is room for laughter at the kings' expense, along with a few sly digs at the pomp of the royal court. The stories' heroes prevail not through physical might or riches but through wit, wisdom, and—most importantly—God's providence. In a context that daily reveals how little the mighty value the lives of those who serve them, such tales reassure the people of Israel that God Almighty has neither forgotten nor abandoned them. The book of Daniel places the stories told by the winners within a larger story that both contextualizes and undercuts them. Nebuchadnezzar is king, yes, but only for a time. There is a Lord greater than Nebuchadnezzar.

In the book of Daniel we first encounter Daniel as a young man. He and his friends Hananiah, Mishael, and Azariah are members of the royal family and the nobility whom "Nebuchadnezzar King of Babel" has brought to "the land of Shinar" (1:1–2), along with Judah's king and the temple vessels. With a few carefully chosen references to Babel and the land of Shinar, the narrator connects Nebuchadnezzar with the tower of Babel, that legendary and failed project of human hubris whose builders said, "Come, let us build ourselves a city, and a tower with its top in the heavens, and let us make a name for ourselves" (Genesis 11:4). Readers familiar with the story know that God thwarted the builders' grand plans and turned their proud speech to babble. By linking Nebuchadnezzar's victory to the tower of Babel, the narrator sets the king's tale of conquest within a larger context that undermines it.

Nebuchadnezzar orders his palace master to select well-educated and wise young men from Judah's nobility. Like the sacrifices offered to the God of Israel and like the priests who serve God, they are to be

without defect. They are to be educated in the language and literature of the king's wise men, fed from the king's table, and trained for
service in the king's court. Among the Judean youths chosen for this
honor are Daniel and his friends, to whom the palace master
promptly gives new names.

Is this renaming significant? Some might say it is an unimportant
detail in the story since, just as students from Japan or China who
attend college in the United States often adopt an English name
because their given names are too difficult for Americans to pronounce, Israelites commonly took a second, foreign name when they
were living among people who did not speak Hebrew. Queen Esther,
for example, is much better known by her foreign name than by her
Hebrew one; although the narrator introduces her
as Hadassah, she is called Esther throughout the
rest of the book. In a number of cases in the Bible
these name changes, like Esther's, are handled mat-
ter-of-factly, without further comment.

Daniel means "God is my judge," Hananiah means "the Lord (Yahweh) is gracious," Mishael means "who is what God is?" and Azariah means "the Lord (Yahweh) has helped."

The situation in Daniel is rather different, however. In the first place, after describing the name
change, the narrator does not immediately begin
using the new names. On the contrary, for the rest
of the chapter he continues to call the four youths by their Hebrew
and not their Babylonian names. Furthermore, the young men's
Hebrew names all honor the God of Israel. As so often occurs in the
Bible, the meaning of the Hebrew names corresponds to the actions
and character of those who bear them. Daniel means "God is my
judge," Hananiah means "the Lord (Yahweh) is gracious," Mishael
means "who is what God is?" and Azariah means "the Lord (Yahweh) has helped." In contrast, their new names honor Babylonian
gods. Abednego, for example, means "Servant of Nabu" (the god of
scribes and writing), and Nebuchadnezzar states that Daniel was
named Belteshazzar "after the name of my god," that is, Bel, another
name for Marduk, the warrior king of the Babylonian pantheon
(4:8). (In the Greek additions to Daniel, Daniel uses a clever strata-
gem to prove that Bel is not a living god.) Finally, the narrator
emphasizes that the young men do not choose the new names for
themselves; instead, they are assigned new names by those in author-

ity over them, whether the palace master or the king. Mandatory name changes are one of the symbolic institutions by which slave societies force slaves to die to their birth identity and be reborn to the identity given them by their master. The master seeks to control every aspect of the slaves' lives; even their names are not their own. Gifts from such a master are never free.

Gifts from the King's Table

Nebuchadnezzar has given Daniel and his friends an elite education, food and wine from the royal table, new names, and the prospect of a place in the royal court. They would appear to be utterly dependent on the king. Daniel, however, refuses to submit to a life completely defined by Nebuchadnezzar. The original Hebrew words of the story make a connection that is not readily apparent in translation: Ashpenaz the palace master "determines" (*yasem*) new names for Daniel and his friends (1:7), but Daniel "determines (*yasem*) in his heart" that he will not defile himself with food and wine from the king's table (1:8).

As even early Jewish commentators noted, the king's gourmet fare was not inherently off limits for Israelites. After all, King Jechoiachin of Judah ate at the Babylonian king's table (2 Kings 25:27–30). Some of the royal food (such as pork and shellfish) would have violated the laws regarding clean and unclean food, but many other dishes would have been regarded as clean. Certainly no biblical law prohibits any Israelite except a Nazirite from drinking wine. If the problem is that the king's food would first have been offered to idols, then the vegetables for the king's table would have been included in the offering, yet Daniel agrees to eat them. So why does he reject the king's delicacies?

One possibility is that the king's rich food and wine were banquet fare, inappropriate for young men sensitive to the captive state of their people. When Nebuchadnezzar's army conquered Judah, they besieged Jerusalem until "the famine became so severe in the city that there was no food for the people of the land," then destroyed the city and burned the temple. They carried all of the remaining population into exile, leaving behind only "some of the poorest people of the land to be vinedressers and tillers of the soil" (2 Kings 25:3, 12). During an earlier period in Israel's history, the prophet Amos pronounced

God's judgment on the nobles and the wealthy who feasted while the common people of their own country suffered:

> Alas for those who lie on beds of ivory,
> and lounge on their couches,
> and eat lambs from the flock,
> and calves from the stall;
> who sing idle songs to the sound of the harp,
> and like David improvise on instruments of music;
> who drink wine from bowls,
> and anoint themselves with the finest oils,
> but are not grieved over the ruin of Joseph!
> Therefore they shall now be the first to go into exile,
> And the revelry of the loungers shall pass away. (Amos 6:4–7)

Unlike the wealthy Israelites of Amos' time, Daniel and his friends refuse to feast when their devastated people are experiencing such famine.

Prophetic texts associate the gluttony of the rich not simply with insensitivity, but also with the oppressive use of power. According to Isaiah, God offers wine and rich fare to the poor at no cost (Isaiah 55:1–3; 25:6). The same could hardly be said of human kings. In the ancient world, the food on the king's table was not for the poor, even though they were the ones who had produced it; instead it came from in-kind taxation of the king's subjects. Much of the meat eaten at royal banquets came from peasants who raised sheep and cattle for wool and milk but considered meat a luxury to be eaten only on rare occasions. As a prayer from Nehemiah, written during the Persian period, describes the situation, "[The land's] rich yield goes to the kings whom you have set over us because of our sins; they have power also over our bodies and over our livestock at their pleasure, and we are in great distress" (Nehemiah 9:37). Given that passages elsewhere in Daniel condemn excessive revelry and emphasize the king's responsibility to provide for all those in his care, Daniel may well be trying to avoid excessive luxury at the expense of the poor during a time of national mourning.

By choosing not to eat the royal fare, Daniel identifies himself more closely with the conquered than with their conqueror. He also clings to his cultural identity. Immigrant peoples keep their culinary traditions long after they have forgotten how to speak the languages of their homelands. How do the Irish in New York celebrate St. Patrick's Day? They may throw around a few Gaelic words, but chiefly they eat corned beef and cabbage and drink (green) beer. Germans in the Midwest celebrate their ethnic heritage with brats and sauerkraut, while Norwegians eat lefse and lutefisk. Mexican immigrants in New Mexico and California gather regularly with family and friends to eat pozole and tamales. The foods we eat help us to remember who we are as a people.

Daniel's desire to avoid defiling himself with the royal food, however, suggests that something more fundamental is also at stake. The word "defile" indicates the need to remain pure, to avoid being contaminated by something unclean. The laws about clean and unclean food were part of an entire system of law that identified the people of Israel as God's own, the people to whom God said, "I am the LORD your God; sanctify yourselves therefore, and be holy, for I am holy" (Leviticus 11:44). Daniel seems to view the delicacies from Nebuchadnezzar's table as unclean not so much because they violate particular kosher laws, but because they threaten his call to be a holy person set apart for a holy God. As Mary Douglas observed in her classic study of the subject, purity laws are an important way in which members of social groups maintain their distinctiveness and avoid being assimilated into the larger culture. Israel's purity laws functioned as boundaries that marked God's people as separate. For Daniel, therefore, eating from the king's hand means that he risks losing his identity as a member of God's holy people, the people of whom God says, "If you obey my voice and keep my covenant, you shall be my treasured possession out of all the peoples. Indeed, the whole earth is mine, but you shall be for me a priestly kingdom and a holy nation" (Exodus 19:5–6).

At the most basic level, the issue at stake is whether Daniel's life will be defined by Nebuchadnezzar or by God. Before him, by Nebuchadnezzar's command, lie the best of food and drink, an elite education, a position of power and prestige,

At the most basic level, the issue at stake is whether Daniel's life will be defined by Nebuchadnezzar or by God. On whom will he depend for food and health and wisdom? Who will be the source of his identity and of his most basic needs?

and the prospect of a privileged and wealthy life. How much is he willing to sacrifice in order to receive what Nebuchadnezzar offers him? To whom will Daniel attribute his success? On whom will he depend for food and health and wisdom? Who will be the source of his identity and of his most basic needs? By choosing to eat vegetables and drink water instead of depending on Nebuchadnezzar's bounty, Daniel demonstrates that he has learned the lesson that God sought to teach the people of Israel during the Exodus:

> [God] humbled you by letting you hunger, then by feeding you with manna, with which neither you nor your ancestors were acquainted, in order to make you understand that one does not live by bread alone, but by every word that comes from the mouth of the LORD. . . . Do not say to yourself, "My power and the might of my own hand have gotten me this wealth." But remember the LORD your God. (Deuteronomy 8:3, 17–18)

Remembering that God, not Nebuchadnezzar, is Lord, Daniel asks Ashpenaz, the palace master, to let him follow his conscience. The Bible records God's response to this request before narrating Ashpenaz's: "Now God gave Daniel kindness and compassion in the presence of the palace master" (our translation). God's gift opens the way for the success of Daniel's request. Ashpenaz is afraid of his lord the king. He worries that his life may be forfeit if Daniel's appearance does not measure up to the others', but he does not outright refuse to do as Daniel asks. Daniel takes this concern into account when he appeals to the guard who has been given responsibility for him and his three friends. He offers a proposal: let the four of them eat a diet of vegetables and water for ten days, then let their appearance be compared with that of the other young men. After ten days, Daniel and his friends appear healthier than all the rest, and "the guard continued to withdraw their royal rations and the wine they were to drink, and gave them vegetables" (1:16). Daniel wisely makes it worth the guard's while to cooperate: Daniel and his friends get vegetables; the guard gets the young men's portion of premium food and wine.

In this chapter, Daniel serves as a teacher and model for Shadrach, Meshach, and Abednego. Nothing indicates that he is older, more trained, or from a more religious family than the others, but he is clearly the leader. In this first story the narrator does not develop the characters of Daniel's friends at all. For example, he does not tell us how Daniel's friends react to having their names changed or what they think of being expected to eat food from the king's table. Daniel speaks and acts, but the others are merely acted upon. We do not hear a single word from them. The narrator does not even tell us whether Daniel consults them before he asks the palace master to feed them a more austere diet. When Daniel includes his friends in this request, however, he opens the way for them to obey God and shows them they have other options besides unquestioning obedience to the king's commands. Thus his actions lead them to mature into independent actors who will demonstrate their own faithfulness to God later in the story.

The four young men continue to prosper without the king's delicacies. Not only do they excel over all the other young men in appearance, but God gives them extraordinary "knowledge and skill in every aspect of literature and wisdom." In the first chapter of Daniel, God appears first and foremost as God the giver—"give" is the only verb associated with God in this chapter. God gives Jehoiakim into Nebuchadnezzar's hand, gives Daniel and his friends kindness and mercy in the presence of Ashpenaz, and gives the four young men knowledge and skill (1:2, 9, 17). Nebuchadnezzar comes, besieges, takes, commands, assigns, speaks, and inquires. God gives, and gives, and gives again. Nebuchadnezzar is front and center as the apparent seat of power. But behind the scenes is God, the source of political power and physical strength, of kindness and mercy, of knowledge and wisdom. Nebuchadnezzar proposes, but God disposes.

At the end of the first chapter, the palace master introduces the young men to Nebuchadnezzar, who finds them to be without peer among all the magicians and enchanters in his kingdom and therefore stations them in his court. Trained in the wisdom both of the Babylonians and of the Jews, they take their place among the scribes and sages who serve the king. In this first test of allegiance, they have found a way to be faithful to God and still serve the king, but their new assignment in the royal court means that they will be more than ever subject to King Nebuchadnezzar's demands. Will it always be possible for them to obey two masters? The stage is set for further tests.

The Challenge of Daniel

The stories in Daniel provide us with a way of imagining the challenges and possibilities that open before us when we seek to serve God above all others. Not all of us are as strong in our faith as Daniel; like Shadrach, Meshach, and Abednego, we may not be equipped to follow God faithfully at first. To a certain extent Daniel as a character in the story represents an ideal, the servant of God who obeys God no matter what the cost. We know that we are not as faithful or as obedient as he is, but a figure like Daniel is not intended to make us feel discouraged. Not at all. Consider, for example, the familiar hymn that many of us sing on All Saints' Day:

> I sing a song of the saints of God,
> Patient and brave and true,
> Who toiled and fought and lived and died
> For the Lord they loved and knew.

The hymn insists that we too can be saints like the heroic figures it celebrates. Similarly, the story of Daniel's life prompts us to consider the difference that it makes in the world when one person truly obeys God. It invites us to imagine: what would happen if I followed God like that? What would the world be like if everyone lived as faithfully as Daniel did? Like Martin Luther King Jr.'s "I Have a Dream" speech, it calls us first to conceive of another possible world and then to dedicate ourselves to making that world a reality.

The book of Daniel portrays God as the one to whom humans owe not only the vision of a better world, but the power to realize that vision. The God who gives Jerusalem into Nebuchadnezzar's hands, who gives the young men discernment and wisdom—this same God is the giver of every resource that human beings need to live. This portrait of God as the creator and sustainer of the world fits well with Israel's wisdom literature. Biblical theologian Walter Brueggemann defines wisdom in Old Testament thought as "the practice of discernment, whereby life is taken as evidence of the demand and gift of Yahweh." Foolishness, by contrast, is "the mistaken sense that one is autonomous and the measure of one's own life."[5] Daniel and his friends wisely recognize that although they might appear to be free to rise to power by serving Nebuchadnezzar, they cannot control their lives by obeying him, nor is he the true source of their identity or of their well-being. A diet of vegetables and water is an effective way to resist the seductive effects of luxury and remind themselves that God is the giver to whom they owe all that they have and all that they are. Their lives depend on God, not on the king.

The concept seems simple enough to grasp, but putting it into practice is not always so simple. As Daniel discovers, sometimes obedience to God leads to earthly rewards that in turn tempt the faithful to disobey God. Daniel's persuasive skills help him to convince his superiors to grant him favors but also leave him socially indebted to those

The kinds of temptations that Daniel and his friends faced in the royal court would have been the stuff of everyday life for the scribes who served in the courts of the Jewish nobility.

who have helped him. His wise choices are rewarded with status, and honor, and greater authority over others. The problem is that along with honor and status come the temptation to pride, and with greater authority comes greater accountability to the king. Furthermore, higher status means higher visibility. Acts that might have seemed unimportant when Daniel and his friends were mere underlings will take on more significance the more powerful that they become. To what extent are Daniel and the others free to serve God? To what extent does their position in the royal court leave them in debt to the king?

The kinds of temptations that Daniel and his friends faced in the royal court would have been the stuff of everyday life for the scribes who served in the courts of the Jewish nobility. The years just before and during the Maccabean revolt were a period rife with political infighting among the elite families in Jerusalem. Members of the nobility competed to win the prized—and profitable—office of royal tax collector. Furthermore, during this period there was little separation between priesthood and politics. Because the Seleucid kings appointed the Jewish high priests, members of the priestly families schemed to win royal favor and be awarded the coveted position.

Some advocated policies designed to please the king, such as transforming Jerusalem into a Hellenistic city complete with a gymnasium, a theater, and a new name that honored the royal family. Others resorted to bribery, traveling to the royal court in Antioch to bring the king tribute money and expensive gifts.

At the same time that the priests and nobility sought the king's favor, they had to avoid offending too many of the Jerusalem elites. Life as a high priest would be impossible, for example, if none of the other priests supported the candidate that the king approved. Successful politicians—and the high priests during the Seleucid era were definitely politicians—need loyal followers if they plan to stay in power. As a result, life in the courts of the Jerusalem nobility was a constant, subtle dance: a graceful bow to royalty here, a generous gesture to a powerful local noble there, two steps sideways to avoid offense, and, if necessary, prostration at the feet of the king.

In the middle of the dance moved the scribes. During this period, few Jews other than the scribes knew how to read. As a result, scribes were the courtiers who wrote and carried messages, the sages who consulted the history books and the stars, and the advisers who helped the nobility to devise the plots and warned them about the possible consequences of their political maneuverings. They were also the scholars entrusted with copying biblical manuscripts and preserving the religious tradition. Since the common people were illiterate, the scribes taught them Israel's religious heritage both by passing on oral traditions and by reading books aloud to them and explaining their meaning.

As we discussed in chapter 1, a group of scribes wrote the book of Daniel. It stands to reason, however, that scribes were also the book's original audience, the readers who introduced the book to everyone else. The authors of the book knew their audience well, and realized that the kinds of dilemmas that Daniel and his friends dealt with in the royal court still plagued sages in their own day. If the high priest and his family began adopting Hellenistic customs that were not entirely in line with Jewish law, should the high priest's sages follow suit? What if they were offered the privilege of eating at the high priest's table? Should they accept the invitation even though they might end up eating questionably kosher food, or food that had been extorted from the poor? Or should they risk alienating their employers by refusing the invitation and eating at home? If they interpreted their religious traditions too strictly, would they forfeit their ability to advocate for policies that benefited the Jewish people? On the other hand, if they interpreted them too loosely, would they cease to be Jews? Then there were the subtler temptations: the lure of praise, the satisfaction of being publicly recognized for a job well done, the seductive appeal of fine clothes and a luxurious lifestyle, beautiful gifts from satisfied employers, and the sheer thrill of private access to the rich and powerful. Day after day, in decisions both big and small, the scribes found themselves caught between the commands of God and the demands of their human superiors.

Although Daniel's life and the lives of the scribes in the royal court may seem foreign to us, the kinds of temptations that they faced are not so different from the ones that we encounter as we seek to serve God not just at church but at work and among our families and friends. In many ways, their dilemma is ours as well. Every Sunday we hear sermons that seek to connect the stories of our lives with the story of God's work in the world. We sing hymns in praise of God's power. During communion we rehearse the history of salvation and are reminded of God's unfathomable love for us. Yet as we move from worship out into the world, we readily discover how easy it is to say, "All things come of Thee, O Lord, and of Thine own have we given Thee," at the same time that our daily lives proclaim the conviction that we are self-made, that our money is ours to use as we wish, and that our deepest allegiances are to the social and economic realities that outwardly determine our work, our social status, and our financial security.

Like Daniel and his friends, and like the scribes for whom the book was first written, we may take a stand on one spiritual or moral issue only to find ourselves tempted to compromise on another. Our lives, our motives, and our relationships are complicated. If we give generously to the church or to charity, for example, we may soon find ourselves more motivated by the honor and praise that we receive for our generosity than we are by our love for God and neighbor. If we hold prominent positions in local service organizations, we may find ourselves entangled in networks of social obligation.

When we receive favors, people expect us to return them, even when what they ask us to do runs counter to our convictions. Daniel's experience foreshadows our own: it is not easy to serve only one lord.

But Daniel's experience also offers hope for our own. No matter how challenging the circumstances, even inexperienced young people in an apparently impossible situation can remain faithful to God. Sometimes the solution is not obvious. Sometimes we may need to use our political skills and worldly wisdom creatively, for divine ends. Although we are responsible for our choices, we cannot predict what the results will be. We may feel like very small players on the world's stage, caught up in events beyond our control. The first chapter of Daniel reminds us that we are characters in God's story, and the end of the story belongs to God.

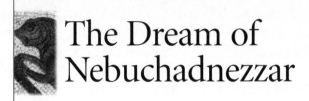 The Dream of Nebuchadnezzar

Have you turned on a television lately, flipped through a magazine, or gone to a website? Wherever we look, we are bombarded by images competing for our attention, competing to express our identity, trying to convince us that they represent our needs, our values, our deepest sense of ourselves. "No fear. . . . Wear the pants. . . . Be all that you can be. . . . It's expensive, but you're worth it!" Sometimes these sales techniques merely reinforce our existing self-images, but sometimes they invite us to ignore the voices of caution and realism and risk a daring step into redefining ourselves: "Wash that gray right out of your hair. . . . Become a new you!" Whether reinforcing or redefining, the ads sell a product by selling a self-image.

At the same time that they play on our sense of ourselves, these ads appeal to our desire to belong to something larger than ourselves. We wash the gray out of our hair so that we will be counted among the young and vital, not the old and irrelevant. We buy the expensive cars and wear the elegant clothes so that we will be accepted in a community where wealth and power go hand in hand. We buy fairly traded and organic products and thus take our place alongside others who are working to establish a just

and sustainable society. Conversely, as we join such groups, our identification with them becomes part of our self-image: "I am a social
progressive," we might say, or "I am a successful banker," or "I am an
economic conservative," or "I am a patron of the arts."

Images and identity are central to the second and third chapters
of Daniel, which both feature stories about images. The first image,
an enormous statue with golden head and clay feet, exists only in
Nebuchadnezzar's dream, while the second—a golden statue to
which all of Nebuchadnezzar's subjects must bow down if they wish
to avoid being thrown into a fiery furnace—is imposingly, fearfully,
present in the real world. The paired stories expose the king's mega-
lomaniacal self-image as well as the extreme measures he is willing
to take to maintain it.

The two tales also invite readers to consider what happens when
competing group memberships reveal conflicting worldviews.
Daniel and the three young men are Jews, but they are also Nebuchadnezzar's advisers. Although they have every reason to value
and preserve their powerful positions in the royal court, at times the
imperial Babylonian worldview and the Jewish worldview are
incompatible. Caught between their dual identities as servants of
God and servants of the king, they compromise when they can, but
take a firm stand when they must.

Two biblical laws are fundamental for understanding these chapters
in Daniel. The first commandment forbids the worship of any god but
Yahweh and the second prohibits making and bowing down to images
(Exodus 20:3–5). Through the stories about images in chapters 2 and
3, the book of Daniel challenges its readers to consider central questions of faith and obedience. It asks, how do images shape human conceptions (and misconceptions) of God? Where is the line between
cultivating self-images and worshipping idols? What does it mean to
serve the one God, the supreme sovereign who rules
over and judges every human sovereign?

> Through the stories about images in chapters 2 and 3, the book of Daniel challenges its readers to consider central questions of faith and obedience.

Nebuchadnezzar's Dream

The book of Daniel portrays King Nebuchadnezzar as a troubled king. It is only the second year of
his reign; he has recently defeated the Assyrians in

the Battle of Carchemish and won the throne. He is immensely wealthy, he wields absolute power in his empire, and servants rush to obey his most trivial commands—yet he can scarcely sleep. His dreams leave him wakeful and afraid. It is unclear whether he even remembers them, but their effect on him is powerful. That is why, sleepless and insecure, he summons "the magicians, the enchanters, the sorcerers, and the Chaldeans ... to tell the king his dreams" (2:2).

The king invites every kind of specialist who might be able to help him, but only the Chaldeans come forward. "Chaldeans" can mean simply Babylonians, but here it refers to a class of sages known for their skill as astrologists. Speaking in Aramaic, the language in which these sections are written, the Chaldeans greet the king with the customary "O king, live forever!" and then offer to interpret his dream—if he will tell them what it is. It is a natural and reasonable request, but Nebuchadnezzar rejects it. Instead he commands them to tell him "both the dream and its interpretation." He promises financial and political reward to anyone who succeeds, but if they fail, he warns, "You shall be torn limb from limb, and your houses shall be laid in ruins" (2:5b).

Not surprisingly, the Chaldeans are perplexed by the king's demand and repeat their request to be told the dream so that they can interpret it, while Nebuchadnezzar in turn accuses them of stalling and of conspiring to lie to him. Perhaps he suspects that they will merely give him a rote answer out of a book, since dream interpretation was so popular in Babylonia that specialists had handbooks with lists of dreams and their interpretations. Interpreting a dream should be an easy task for a Chaldean, but telling the king not only the interpretation, but the dream itself, is beyond their ability. Mystified and terrified, the Chaldeans tell Nebuchadnezzar that he is being unreasonable, for only the gods, "whose dwelling is not with mortals," are capable of telling the king what he dreamed. As far as the Chaldeans are concerned, the gods are too remote to care about human affairs. Divine help is out of the question, and the king is out of luck.

The Chaldeans' reply infuriates Nebuchadnezzar. He may be worried about the ripple effects of their refusal to give him what he wants, since like many monarchs before and after him, Nebuchadnezzar cannot afford to tolerate disobedience. In a violent rage he orders the execution not only of the Chaldeans, but of all the sages in Babylon. The violence of his reaction is telling. This is not a king who has won the hearts and minds of his people. He cannot afford to relax— any sign of weakness, any moment of inattention, opens him to an attempt on his throne and his life. Nebuchadnezzar maintains his position through force. It is not surprising, then, that he has such fearful dreams. What tyrant can rest easy when he knows that he controls his domain only because he has terrified his subjects into submission?

No doubt the king realizes that he cannot rule well without his expert advisers and that his order to execute "all the wise men of Babylon" is self-defeating; only fools will be left to advise the king. Nebuchadnezzar, however, is trapped by his own threats. He demands absolute obedience from his counselors, but they cannot give it because they are unable to tell him his dream. Only the gods, they insist, are able to do what he asks, and not even Nebuchadnezzar can command the gods. Ultimately he too is mortal. Wise courtiers may greet him by saying, "O king, live forever," but he knows that he will not. The Chaldeans have confronted him with his limits, and he cannot bear the truth of their words. Furthermore, he has threatened them with a horrible death, so how can he save face if he allows his advisers to live? What power does he have apart from the promise of reward and the fear of death? Caught in a dilemma of his own devising, Nebuchadnezzar issues the command, and the search for the sages, including Daniel and his companions, begins.

When Daniel learns about the peril that they face, he discreetly asks Arioch, the king's executioner, for more information about Nebuchadnezzar's decree. As soon as he understands the situation, he approaches the king and promises to interpret the dream. Since, like the Chaldeans who enraged the king, Daniel asks for time to complete the task, it seems surprising that the king grants his request. Apparently God has given Daniel "grace and mercy" in the eyes not only of the palace master (cf. 1:9), but of Nebuchadnezzar himself. It is worth noting that Daniel claims that he can do something that, according to the Chaldeans, is possible only for the gods. If the Chaldeans are right, then Daniel must be an emissary of the gods.

Their apparent willingness to give Nebuchadnezzar what he asks, therefore, affirms the king's belief in his own vast importance and presents him with a safe way out of the trap.

Readers of Scripture may notice the parallels between this story and that of Joseph in Egypt interpreting Pharaoh's dreams. Both men are Jews, brought to a foreign country against their will. Because God showers grace and mercy on both captives, they both receive special favor from those in charge of their care, whether the palace master or, in Joseph's case, the chief jailor. In both cases the supreme ruler is troubled by an inexplicable dream; both kings consult their magicians and wise men, but not even their most skilled interpreters can interpret the dreams. Eventually the wise Jew is brought to the king's attention. Both Joseph and Daniel insist that the interpretation of dreams belongs to God (Joseph answers Pharaoh, "It is not I; God will give Pharaoh a favorable answer," while Daniel tells the king, "There is a God in heaven who reveals mysteries, and he has disclosed to King Nebuchadnezzar what will happen"); and both kings reward the dream interpreters by promoting them to positions of power.

The two stories resemble in each other not only in details like these, but also in their insistence that although humans may appear to control events, behind the scenes it is God who truly directs the action. For example, when Jacob's sons discover that the brother they sold into slavery is now second in command in Egypt, they quite naturally fear that he will use his newfound power to retaliate against them. Contrary to all that they might expect, Joseph tells them, "Do not be distressed, or angry with yourselves, because you sold me here; for God sent me before you to preserve life" (Genesis 45:5). After Jacob's death, Joseph once again assures his brothers that he forgives them: "Even though you intended to do harm to me, God intended it for good, in order to preserve a numerous people, as he is doing today" (50:20). God's intervention has brought lifesaving results out of their death-dealing actions.

Furthermore, as the stories of Joseph and Daniel emphasize, God has compassion and concern for all nations, not just for Israel. By interpreting the dreams, Joseph saves the Egyptians as well as his

As the stories of Joseph and Daniel emphasize, God has compassion and concern for all nations, not just for Israel.

own family from dying of hunger, and Daniel saves not only himself and his friends but all the Babylonian sages from execution. Furthermore, Daniel's behavior immediately after he leaves the king's presence accentuates the importance of this theme. He asks only Hananiah, Mishael, and Azariah "to seek mercy from the God of heaven concerning this mystery," but the reason for the prayer is so that he and his companions "with the rest of the wise men of Babylon might not perish" (2:18). Daniel asks his friends to pray that God's mercy will extend not just to them, but to all the sages.

By asking them to pray, Daniel continues to encourage his friends to grow as people of faith and eventual leaders. In the first chapter, he mentored them by showing them how to negotiate an arrangement that would satisfy the king's demands without sacrificing their religious identity. Now, instead of suggesting that they beg the king not to kill them, he tells them to seek mercy from God. When they pray, they act on their faith that their lives depend not on Nebuchadnezzar, but on God. God's answer will deepen their faith and prepare them to act independently of Daniel in the next chapter, when they will have to choose between bowing down to the golden statue and being thrown into the fiery furnace. In this passage the narrator identifies Daniel's friends by their Hebrew names, Hananiah ("Yahweh is gracious"), Mishael ("who is what God is?"), and Azariah ("Yahweh has helped"). As if to echo the meanings of their names, God grants the young men grace and help by revealing the mystery to Daniel in a night vision.

In response to God's gift, Daniel blesses the God of heaven as the one to whom wisdom and power belong, the transcendent God who changes the times and seasons. The God of heaven is sovereign over history, deposing kings and setting up kings. Unlike the Chaldeans' gods, however, the God whom Daniel serves is accessible, revealing "deep and hidden things," making divine wisdom and power available to mortals such as Daniel. God is both far off and near at hand, not only the eternal God of unimaginable might, but also the God who is intimately concerned with human history, who answers prayer and meets human needs. Because the God of Israel graciously reveals the mystery, Daniel is able to interpret the king's dream and thereby save himself, his friends, and all the sages of Babylon.

The narrator's description of the next scene is rather disconcerting, for when Arioch the executioner, at Daniel's request, brings him before Nebuchadnezzar, it is as though the king has never seen him before. The scene contributes to the narrator's portrait of the king as erratic and unpredictable. Perhaps loss of sleep has led to loss of memory. In any case, Arioch tells Nebuchadnezzar that he has "found among the exiles from Judah a man who can tell the king the interpretation." Nebuchadnezzar responds with a question that clarifies the difficulty of Daniel's task: "Are you able to tell me *the dream that I have seen* and its interpretation?" (2:25b–26; emphasis ours). The interpretation alone will not suffice.

Daniel, knowing what he is about to tell the king, omits the usual courteous greeting. Given the content of the dream, he cannot honestly say, "O king, live forever." He begins by reminding Nebuchadnezzar of the truth that the Chaldeans have told him: no mortal, however wise and learned, can reveal the mystery to the king. Daniel, however, has more to offer than the Chaldeans did, because "there is a God in heaven who reveals mysteries" (2:28). He explains that God has revealed the mystery to him not because he is exceptionally wise, but because God wishes to help the king understand his thoughts. Then Daniel describes Nebuchadnezzar's dream:

> You were looking, O king, and lo! there was a great statue. This statue was huge, its brilliance extraordinary; it was standing before you, and its appearance was frightening. The head of that statue was of fine gold, its chest and arms of silver, its middle and thighs of bronze, its legs of iron, its feet partly of iron and partly of clay. (2:31–33)

Then a stone "cut out, not by human hands" pulverized the statue so completely that the wind carried away the shattered bits of gold, silver, bronze, iron, and clay. Not a trace of the statue remained, and afterwards, the stone became a mountain that filled the earth.

After describing the dream, Daniel immediately begins to interpret it. The "head of gold" represents none other than Nebuchadnezzar himself. "You, O king," begins Daniel,

> the king of kings—to whom the God of heaven has given the kingdom, the power, the might, and the glory, into whose hand he has given human beings, wherever they live, the wild animals of the field, and the

birds of the air, and whom he has established as ruler over them all—
you are the head of gold. (2:37–38)

Daniel's words repeatedly emphasize Nebuchadnezzar's exceptional status as "king of kings" and the power that he wields over all. Such immense, imposing statues of gods and kings were a familiar feature of the ancient world. The Greek historian Herodotus, who lived a century after the historical Nebuchadnezzar, describes a shrine in Babylon that contained a twenty-foot solid gold image of Zeus. He also mentions enormous statues of kings, such as a fifty-foot statue of the Egyptian King Sesostris and his wife. Like the monuments of Egypt or triumphal arches of Rome, such statues were meant to impress viewers with the power and permanence of the regimes that put them in place.

At first, Daniel's interpretation of Nebuchadnezzar's dream seems consistent with such a vision of power and permanence. After all, the head of gold is Nebuchadnezzar himself. But Daniel goes on to explain that the parts of the statue below Nebuchadnezzar's "head of gold" represent three, progressively weaker, kingdoms that will rule after him. Together with the golden head, they will be destroyed by an eternal kingdom established by the God of heaven.

Daniel's dream interpretation raises questions for us as we try to understand its significance for its first readers. Does the vision have to do with the end times, or with historical events beginning in Nebuchadnezzar's reign?

Daniel's dream interpretation raises several questions for us as we try to understand its significance for its first readers. First, does the vision have to do with the end times, or with historical events beginning in Nebuchadnezzar's reign? Why is Nebuchadnezzar identified as the head of gold, and which kingdoms do the other parts of the statue represent? Finally, who or what is the stone "cut out, not by human hands"?

Daniel tells the king that God has disclosed what will take place "at the end of days" (2:28, NRSV) or "in days to come" (NIV). The two translations lead to quite different understandings of the dream's meaning. The first suggests that the vision is a prophecy of the end times, the end of history; the second suggests that it is merely about events in the near future. It is important to note that the word that NRSV translates as "end" often means simply "hereafter" or "the future," and elsewhere it translates the Hebrew equivalent of "at the end of days" as "in days to come" (Genesis 49:1 and Numbers 24:14). Given the context and the most common meaning of the phrase, the NIV translation "in days to come" is more accurate. The vision is not about the end of the world, but about a succession of historical kings or kingdoms beginning in Nebuchadnezzar's own time.

The fact that Nebuchadnezzar himself is the head of gold provides further evidence that the dream refers to events within history rather than beyond it, but what does this suggest about the king? Gold is the most valuable and beautiful of the statue's components, so the interpretation might seem to cast Nebuchadnezzar in a positive light. Since Nebuchadnezzar constructs an entire golden statue in the next chapter, it is clear that the king understands the dream as affirming him and his power. The first readers of Daniel, however, would probably have viewed the symbolism of the golden head far less positively—after all, where did ancient kings get the gold and other precious metals for their massive monuments? They demanded it in payment of taxes or seized it from other nations as booty in war. After Nebuchadnezzar conquered Jerusalem, the bronze pillars of the temple were broken in pieces and carried to Babylon along with the silver and gold, and the very first verses of Daniel tell the reader that Nebuchadnezzar brought the temple treasures to Babylon. So when Nebuchadnezzar and gold are mentioned in the same context, how could the people of Judah help but think of the gold stolen from the house of God in Jerusalem?

If Nebuchadnezzar, the preeminent Babylonian king, is the golden head, what does the rest of the statue represent? Elsewhere in Daniel we are told that Darius the Mede conquered Babylon and was succeeded by Cyrus the Persian. This account of history does not agree with other biblical accounts of the period or with historical documents found outside the Bible, but it is the book of Daniel's rendering of the succession of empires. If we follow this historical framework, the silver chest and arms represent the Medes and King Darius, and the bronze middle and thighs represent the Persians and King Cyrus. The fourth kingdom, then, would be the Greeks.

Associating the iron and clay with the Greeks makes sense of several important details in the biblical text. In the days of Alexander the Great, the Greek (Hellenistic) empire crushed and shattered all the other empires, but the legs of iron quickly deteriorated, becoming "partly of iron and partly of clay" after Alexander's death, when his kingdom was divided among his successors. The ancient homeland of the Jews became a meeting ground—and at times a battleground—between two of the dynasties founded by Alexander's successors. Sometimes the Ptolemies ruled Jerusalem from Egypt; at other times the Seleucids ruled Jerusalem from Syria. The historical situation fits well with Daniel's words: "As you saw the iron mixed with clay, so will they mix with one another in marriage, but they will not hold together, just as iron does not mix with clay" (2:43). Mixed but not bonded, the Ptolemies and Seleucids alternately fought with each other and tried to keep the peace through marriage alliances.

The head of gold is the only feature of the statue that Daniel identifies precisely, and Nebuchadnezzar fixes on this detail of the dream. Nevertheless, within both the dream and its interpretation the emphasis falls on the feet of iron mixed with clay and on the destruction of the statue by the stone that grows into a mountain. On the most basic level, the dream undercuts royal delusions of grandeur much like the ending of Percy Bysshe Shelley's poem "Ozymandias":

> My name is Ozymandias, king of kings:
> Look upon my works, ye Mighty, and despair!"
>   Nothing beside remains. Round the decay
> Of that colossal wreck, boundless and bare
> The lone and level sands stretch far away.

As the relentless march of time and the sands of many seasons fell the mighty ruler's monument to his own magnificence, an even more dramatic force fells the statue in Nebuchadnezzar's dream—gold, silver, bronze, iron, and clay are all destroyed by a single stone.

If no human hands have cut the stone, from whence does it come? It is sent by the God of heaven, the Lord of history, the God who "changes times and seasons, deposes kings and sets up kings" (2:21). The description of the stone as "cut out not by human hands" distinguishes it from the idols of the nations, which the Bible frequently caricatures as "silver and gold, the work of human hands" (Psalm

115:4 and 135:15). The prophet Isaiah mocks those who worship such idols:

> they hire a goldsmith, who makes it into a god;
>   then they fall down and worship!
> They lift it to their shoulders, they carry it,
>   they set it in its place, and it stands there;
>   it cannot move from its place.
> If one cries out to it, it does not answer
>   or save anyone from trouble. (Isaiah 46:6–7)

The God of Israel stands in dramatic contrast to idols made from metal or stone by human hands. David asks, "For who is God, but the LORD? And who is a rock, except our God?" and the Bible often refers to God as a rock, steadfast and sure. In Daniel's interpretation of Nebuchadnezzar's vision, however, the stone does not represent God, for the phrase "not with human hands" emphasizes its divine origin without associating it directly with God's own being. Instead the stone is an *agent* through which God demonstrates divine lordship over history, crushing all the kingdoms represented by the statue. The original readers of Daniel would have understood the stone as referring first and foremost to God's judgment of earthly kings such as Nebuchadnezzar and Antiochus IV Epiphanes. As such, the destruction of the statue is a powerful vision of hope: the king under whose tyranny they suffer is accountable to God. From the perspective of Daniel's readers, the kingdoms of Nebuchadnezzar and his successors had already fallen. At present Antiochus IV Epiphanes might seem invulnerable, but according to the dream interpretation he was the weakest part of the statue, the feet of mixed iron and clay. Although his human subjects felt powerless before him, he would be brought down by God's command.

Although Antiochus IV Epiphanes might seem invulnerable, according to the dream interpretation he was the weakest part of the statue, the feet of mixed iron and clay.

The first readers of Daniel looked forward not just to the downfall of Antiochus, but to the new era that would follow. After the stone destroys the statue, it grows into a mountain, symbolizing the kingdom that God will set up (2:44–45). Some of the first readers thought of the kingdom in purely human, political terms. They saw the people of Israel as the earthly embodiment of God's kingdom, a view that is reflected both in the Dead Sea Scrolls and in the words that the crowds cry out two centuries later when Jesus enters Jerusalem: "Hosanna! Blessed is the one who comes in the name of the Lord! Blessed is the coming kingdom of our ancestor David!" (Mark 11:9–10). The scribal authors of Daniel, however, viewed the kingdom as having both a temporal and an eternal aspect. It begins in the days of the kingdoms symbolized by the statue, but continues forever and grows to fill the whole earth. The overall point communicated by the dream and its interpretation comes through clearly, as Daniel shows us the God "who changes times and seasons, deposes kings and sets up kings" (2:21). The God of heaven destroys delusions and reshapes human lives. The stone that pulverizes the statue makes room for a new vision of the kingdom of God, a domain of peace and justice in which the mighty are brought low and the humble are lifted up.

When Daniel has finished interpreting Nebuchadnezzar's dream, the king not only falls on his face to worship Daniel, but commands that he be offered a grain offering and an incense offering. Then Nebuchadnezzar acclaims Daniel's God as "God of gods and Lord of kings," showers Daniel with gifts, and promotes Daniel to a position of authority over the whole province of Babylon and all the other wise men. At Daniel's request, he also promotes Daniel's friends Shadrach, Meshach, and Abednego. This is not the reaction one might expect from someone who has just been told that he, the head of gold, will be destroyed along with all his earthly accomplishments.

Nebuchadnezzar's confession of God's lordship is striking. Where else in the Hebrew Bible do we see a pagan king so openly acknowledging the God of Israel as ruler of gods and kings? As events in the next chapter will show, however, Nebuchadnezzar's words certainly do not represent a genuine change of heart, but merely a response to superior power. Nebuchadnezzar acknowledges the God who guided Daniel to describe and interpret his dream, and his reaction is at best a partial, strategic, self-seeking manipulation of the situation. It is designed to win favor and ward off disaster. Perhaps it is even Nebuchadnezzar's attempt to get Daniel's God on his side.

In such circumstances it is not particularly strange that the king would treat Daniel with the reverence due to a god. After all, Daniel has accomplished what all of the king's advisors have told him only a god could do. Nebuchadnezzar rightly recognizes a divine hand at work here, even if he mistakenly worships the messenger rather than God who sent him. In a sense, he is trying to worship God by worshipping Daniel—an almost comical act of idolatry to those familiar with Mosaic law. More surprising by far than Nebuchadnezzar's act of worship is the fact that the biblical text gives no indication that Daniel refuses Nebuchadnezzar's offerings or expresses any discomfort about being worshiped.

It is instructive to compare Daniel's behavior with the reactions of Peter, Paul, and Barnabas under similar circumstances. In the book of Acts, when Cornelius falls at Peter's feet and begins to worship him, Peter tells the centurion, "Stand up; I am only a mortal" (Acts 10:26) and makes him get up. Later, after Paul has healed a man crippled from birth, the people of the city hail Barnabas as Zeus and Paul as Hermes and try to offer sacrifices to them. Paul and Barnabas' response is dramatic: "They tore their clothes and rushed out into the crowd, shouting, 'Friends, why are you doing this? We are mortals just like you, and we bring you good news, that you should turn from these worthless things to the living God'" (Acts 14:14–15). By contrast, although Daniel claims to serve the God of heaven, he does nothing to prevent the king from worshipping God's messenger instead. How can it be that a man like Daniel accepts worship that belongs to God alone? Although Daniel is exceptionally wise, the narrator of these stories also presents him as genuinely human, vulnerable to the temptations of praise and power. Apparently, when the king falls at his feet and offers sacrifice, Daniel is carried away by a sense of his own importance. Soon all his peers in the royal court will know that he has done what they claim only the gods can do.

Both the scribal authors and the scribes who first read and interpreted their work for others would have been familiar with the drive to stand out from the crowd and the temptation to take credit for wisdom that was not really theirs. Courtiers' livelihoods depend on their reputations for exceptional political skill, intelligence, and insight. The authors turn the character of Daniel into a mirror that reflects the scholarly hunger for success and recognition and reveals the danger that sages run when they compromise their principles in order to feed their egos.

If Daniel thinks that he truly deserves the honor that Nebuchadnezzar offers him, then the interpreter of the dream has succumbed to the voice of his own pride and forgotten the dream's essential point: the kingdom, the power, the might, and the glory may be entrusted to humans for a time, but ultimately they belong to God alone. His self-image has become distorted to such an extreme that, like Nebuchadnezzar's, it has become an idol. By accepting Nebuchadnezzar's obeisance before him, Daniel prefigures the megalomania that will overcome the king in the next chapter.

The Golden Idol

Nebuchadnezzar's acknowledgement of God as "Lord of kings" at the end of chapter 2 suggests that he has understood Daniel's interpretation of the dream. His behavior in chapter 3, however, demonstrates that although he may have gotten the message, he has missed its meaning: he erects a golden statue and requires all his subjects to bow down before it or else be thrown into the fiery furnace. Daniel has told him that he is the head of gold to whom God has given authority to rule, but the king promptly misconstrues this image, focusing on the golden symbol of his own greatness and conveniently forgetting that the whole statue will eventually be destroyed.

The two stories about statues in Daniel reveal the formative character of dreams, images, and symbols of power. Within Nebuchadnezzar coexist the unquenchable desire for power and the hidden fear that flows from knowing that he is human, limited and, like the lowliest slaves in his kingdom, ultimately powerless to prevent his own death. Suppressing his fear, Nebuchadnezzar seeks to embody his mental image of power by constructing a physical image, a golden statue before which all will be compelled to prostrate themselves. Given that, like the head of the dream statue, the image is made of gold, the statue probably represents the king himself. This monstrous monument to Nebuchadnezzar's ego is sixty cubits in height and six cubits in width, or about ninety feet tall and nine feet wide. Gleaming golden in the sun, towering over the people below, it is meant to be an imposing sight.

In the ancient world such statues were symbols both of state religion and of royal power. At public occasions such as the dedication festival that Nebuchadnezzar announces in Daniel 3, all the king's subjects would be expected to fall down before the statue. Their obeisance signified not only worship of a divine being, but submission to the king and participation in the value system of the state. If chapter 2 presupposes that the stability of the state depends on obedient courtiers, chapter 3 shows that it also depends on a submissive populace. The more insecure the king, the more insatiable is his desire to have his power reaffirmed by his subjects. Public displays of loyalty strengthen the king's authority and control over his kingdom, while any disloyalty opens the way for others to imagine that they too might choose to resist the king's will.

> *All the king's subjects would be expected to fall down before the statue, signifying not only worship of a divine being, but submission to the king and participation in the value system of the state.*

This depiction of Nebuchadnezzar as a violent king who claims divine prerogatives and imposes fearsome punishments on those who resist his will would have resonated strongly with the book's first audience, Jews suffering under the tyranny of the Syrian king Antiochus IV Epiphanes. Antiochus was called "Epiphanes" because he claimed to be an "epiphany" of God, that is, God manifest. Like Nebuchadnezzar, he expected to be worshipped as a god. According to 1 and 2 Maccabees, when Antiochus celebrated his birthday, he compelled the Jews to participate in a festival honoring the Greek god Dionysus and to offer sacrifices to him. He also prohibited burnt offerings and sacrifices to Yahweh and commanded the Jews "to profane sabbaths and festivals, to defile the sanctuary and the priests, to build altars and sacred precincts and shrines for idols, to sacrifice swine and other unclean animals, and to leave their sons uncircumcised" (1 Maccabees 1:45b–48). Death was the penalty for resistance. As the books of the Maccabees record, some were tortured to death on the rack for refusing to eat pork and others burned alive for observing the Sabbath. Women who dared to circumcise their children in defiance of the king's command were paraded around the city with their babies at their breasts, and then both the mothers and the babies were thrown to their deaths from the city wall.

Because they lived under the tyranny of a brutal king, the first readers of Daniel would have found Nebuchadnezzar's fiery penalty for disobedience entirely credible. They might have been taken off guard at first, though, by the over-the-top pomp of the herald's announcement (3:4) and the literary style of the story that follows. The entire chapter is packed with detailed lists and repeated, ornate phrases. For example, Nebuchadnezzar sends for "the satraps, the prefects, and the governors, the counselors, the treasurers, the justices, the magistrates, and all the officials of the provinces." Variants of the phrase "the golden statue that King Nebuchadnezzar has set up" occur eight times in just seventeen verses (3:2–18). Similarly, the furnace is never just a furnace: it is always "a furnace of blazing fire."

Ancient kings were prone to issue statements filled with self-aggrandizing language and long lists of royal titles. But in Daniel 3 the narrator satirizes the familiar, flowery language of the imperial court by carrying it to an extreme, with devastating results. For anyone who reads the story or hears it read aloud, the cumulative effect of so much pomp is comical, and for people in Daniel's day, it would have been both hilarious and therapeutic. The style of the storytelling subverts Nebuchadnezzar's authority. For Daniel's readers, it also undercuts Antiochus' because, without stating his name, it mocks his ridiculous claim to be God manifest. Both kings' pretensions to absolute power are serious, but it becomes impossible for the reader to take them seriously. How can one cower and laugh at the same time? Humor rehumanizes the king; turning him into an object of satire makes it possible for his subjects to imagine that they can resist his will.

Immediately after the herald's announcement, the narrator records the prompt response of Nebuchadnezzar's subjects to the king's decree: "As soon as all the peoples heard the sound of the horn, pipe, lyre, trigon, harp, drum, and entire musical ensemble, all the peoples, nations, and languages fell down and worshiped the golden statue that King Nebuchadnezzar had set up" (3:7). It would appear that the king's threat has had the desired effect.

But has it? As some Chaldeans are quick to inform the king (after first reminding him at length and in detail about the death penalty that he has established for disobedience to his decree), there are certain troublesome Jews—more specifically, Shadrach, Meshach, and Abednego—who refuse to worship the golden statue no matter how impressive the musical ensemble may be, and even though everyone else is doing it. As the Chaldeans are also quick to point out, these are the very people "whom you have appointed over the affairs of the province of Babylon." Surprisingly, they do not mention Daniel, who presumably also has refused to worship the golden statue. But he will face his own test of loyalty in chapter 6, and the focus now is on Daniel's protégés. In any case, the Chaldeans not-so-subtly suggest that the king has made a mistake by giving these Jews a position of such authority, for not only do they refuse to worship the golden statue, but they do not serve Nebuchadnezzar's gods. Nor do they limit themselves to reporting the facts. They frame the Jews' refusal to worship idols as just one symptom of a more serious disease: these foreigners pay no heed to the king.

Nebuchadnezzar responds to the Chaldeans' accusations with all the rage of a tyrant who feels his power thwarted and his claims to ultimacy denied. He orders Shadrach, Meshach, and Abednego brought before him and demands to know whether the charges are true. Do they indeed not serve his gods? Do they indeed refuse to worship the golden statue that he has set up? Interestingly, he says nothing about the Chaldeans' claim that the young men pay no heed to the king. Perhaps he thinks that he can determine the truth by observing their reaction to his intimidating rage. He offers them one last opportunity to submit to his authority: if they bow at the sound of his music, they will live; if they refuse to worship the golden statue, they will die an immediate, fiery death. By his command they will live or die, "and who," he asks, "is the god that will deliver you out of my hands?" Apparently Nebuchadnezzar has forgotten all about the God whom he praised in the previous chapter as "God of gods and Lord of kings." When he feels his power threatened, this king acknowledges no Lord greater than himself.

Shadrach, Meshach, and Abednego answer with one voice, addressing Nebuchadnezzar without flattery, without wishes for his long life, without even the title of "king." In this brief speech, the only words that they speak in the entire book, they show no fear. They deny the king even the satisfaction of watching them try to defend themselves against the charges. Nebuchadnezzar has asked what he sees as a rhetorical question: "And who is the god that will deliver you out of my hands?" The young men give him an unexpectedly direct answer: "If our God whom we serve is able to deliver us from the furnace of blazing fire and out of your hand, O king, let him deliver us. But if not, be it known to you, O king, that we will not serve your gods" (3:15, 17–18). They do not set up a false image by insisting that to be worthy of worship God must protect them from all harm. Their obedience to God is not contingent on rescue. If God delivers them, so be it. If God does not, so be it. Regardless, they will not serve the king's gods, nor will they worship the golden statue that he has set up.

Confronted with the young men's steadfast refusal to bow to his image, Nebuchadnezzar is "so filled with rage" that, according to the literal meaning of the Aramaic, "the image of his face changed."

Confronted with the young men's steadfast refusal to bow to his image, Nebuchadnezzar is "so filled with rage" that, according to the literal meaning of the Aramaic, "the image of his face changed." The word translated here as "image" is the same word used to describe the statue. The king's idolatrous self-image is threatened, and he must find a way to save face. He is overcome with fury because he worships his own power, but these three Jews will not, and he is helpless to change their behavior. If he cannot terrify Shadrach, Meshach, and Abednego into bowing down to his image, what option does he have left except to kill them?

The biblical text emphasizes the king's fury by using exaggeration—determined to prove he wields the power of life and death, Nebuchadnezzar orders the fiery furnace superheated to seven times its usual temperature. He commands the strongest guards in his army to bind the young men, although nothing in the text indicates that the prisoners attempt to defend themselves in any way. On the contrary, they remain silent, submitting themselves utterly to the will of the God whom they serve. The king, desperate to be obeyed absolutely and immediately, utterly disregards the safety of his guards. His obedient servants are killed by the same raging flames into which they throw the three disobedient Jews. Shadrach, Meshach, and Abednego fall down, fully clothed, bound, and silent, into the fiery furnace. The Aramaic text makes the allusion clear:

because of their refusal to "fall down" before the image, the three young men "fell down" into the fire.

The version found in the Septuagint focuses on the young men's experiences in the furnace. They walk around in the fire singing and praising God, and Azariah (Abednego) prays a penitential prayer from the midst of the flames. The Greek version also includes a colorful description of Nebuchadnezzar's servants stoking the fire at the same time that the angel of the Lord comes down into the furnace to accompany the young men and protect them from harm. Then Hananiah, Mishael, and Azariah bless God the creator as the ruler of all, the source of all life, and the merciful one who saves them from the power of death (the "Song of the Three Young Men" in the Book of Common Prayer).

But in the more familiar (Aramaic) version of the story, we view the episode in the fiery furnace only through Nebuchadnezzar's eyes. Incredulous, the king seeks verification from his counselors: three bound men were thrown into the fire, were they not? Then why are four unbound men walking around in the middle of the fire, unhurt, and why does one of them look like a divine being? Puzzled and amazed, the king approaches the door of the furnace and issues a command: "Shadrach, Meshach, and Abednego, servants of the Most High God, come out!" Three men fall down into the fire, and three men come out unharmed. The fourth appears only in the midst of the flames. A comprehensive assembly of government officials bears witness to the incredible scene that unfolds before Nebuchadnezzar: the fire has been powerless to hurt these men; their hair and their clothing remain unscathed; they do not even smell of smoke.

Nebuchadnezzar reacts dramatically to the young men's emergence from the fire, saying, "Blessed be the God of Shadrach, Meshach, and Abednego, who has sent his angel and delivered *his servants* who trust in him" (v. 28, emphasis ours). The fact that Abednego's name appears last in the list highlights the Jews' true allegiance: the young man whom the palace master has named "Servant of Nebo" is in fact a servant of the God of Israel. His Hebrew name is Azariah, "Yahweh has helped," and the story proves the truth of that name. God does not spare the young men from walking through the fire, but God is with them in the midst of the flames, and they are not consumed. Although Nebuchadnezzar had demanded to know, "Who is the god that will deliver you out of my hands?" ultimately the young men never were in his hands. They were in God's hands all along.

The reassurance of God's presence in the midst of suffering was a powerful word for Jews who were suffering persecution under Antiochus IV Epiphanes. They turned to the stories of Daniel and of the three young men to help them find the courage to remain faithful to God even though it meant facing excruciating pain and death. As 1 Maccabees puts it, "Hananiah, Azariah, and Mishael believed and were saved from the flame. Daniel, because of his innocence, was delivered from the mouth of the lions. And so observe, from generation to generation, that none of those who put their trust in him will lack strength" (1 Maccabees 2:59–61). The author of 1 Maccabees does not promise that God will always choose to deliver those who put their trust in God. He promises only that God's strength will be enough for them.

His interpretation of the story does justice to the three young men's final words to Nebuchadnezzar: whether or not God delivers them, they will not serve other gods. The theological point of their response is that humans do not control God. If they did, God would be neither sovereign nor free. Such a god would be merely another idol created in our image. The God whom Daniel and his friends worship is accessible, but not manipulable.

The attitude of Daniel and his friends stands in stark contrast to Nebuchadnezzar's. The king's final words in chapter 3 demonstrate that although he recognizes God as the one who is able to deliver, he does not understand that his own authority to rule depends on God's permissive will. His order appears to honor God, but in reality it is merely another attempt to establish his own preeminence. He does not retract the law that commands all people everywhere to worship the image that he has set up. Instead, the king issues a decree that any who utter blasphemy against the young men's God are to be dismembered, and their houses destroyed. The absurd violence of the command shows that Nebuchadnezzar still perceives himself as the one who wields the power of life and death, the absolute ruler who controls the religious behavior of his subjects.

The king has not learned his lesson. He continues to worship his own image.

The three young men have resisted the king and survived. They have even been promoted. But like Daniel's dream interpretation in the previous chapter, their message has fallen on ears so deaf that it came through only in distorted form. Because the monarch's worldview remains unchanged, their position in the king's court is no less precarious than it was before. They have been delivered out of the fire back into the frying pan. Like the scribes serving in the courts of nobles in Antiochus IV's day, they must navigate two very different worlds at the same time.

> To the scribes fell the delicate task of balancing flattery and wise counsel while keeping both their masters' egos and their own in check. Where was the line between prudence and faithlessness?

Jewish nobles as well as Babylonian and Greek ones were apt to make themselves objects of worship. To the scribes fell the delicate task of balancing flattery and wise counsel while keeping both their masters' egos and their own in check. Their task must have been especially difficult if they served noble families who were seeking Antiochus' favor. When a Jewish noble ordered his scribe to write a letter addressed to King Antiochus, "god manifest," should the faithful scribe accept the wording and write the letter, or not? If the noble told the scribe that owning a copy of the Torah was punishable by death, and then asked whether to destroy the family's scrolls, what could the scribe say? Where was the line between prudence and faithlessness? Which convictions were worth dying for? In such a context, what did being faithful look like, and why would God's people choose to remain loyal to God despite the tremendous cost?

The book of Daniel depicts the relationship between God and God's people as fundamentally different from the relationships between human rulers and their subjects. Human sovereigns control the population of their realms by fear, by gratitude, or by creating a clientele financially or socially indebted to them. They not infrequently resort to desperate measures in their attempts to control the lives of the people within their domain and to possess their goods and their loyalty. Such efforts to establish total dominion paradoxically exhibit profound weakness by revealing the utter dependency of the rulers on the very people they seek to control. What good is a sovereign without subjects?

By contrast, although God delivers Daniel as well as Daniel's companions, the story makes it quite clear that their loyalty does not depend on that deliverance. The God whom they serve evokes love, awe, and wonder, a response more profound and lasting than terror or obligation. They obey God neither from fear of punishment, nor from desire for reward, but simply because God is God, holy, beautiful, and worthy of worship. In return for their loyalty, God offers no guarantee that they will be spared from suffering or even from death. Nevertheless, in the moment of their deepest need, they encounter the most profound reality of all. In the midst of the fire, God is with them, and that is enough.

These chapters of Daniel show us a God both intimate and transcendent, the divine presence from whom we can neither hide nor escape, the eternal source of wisdom and power who remains always beyond our grasp. Like Nebuchadnezzar, like Daniel, we readily fall into the trap of serving other gods by transforming ourselves into objects of worship. Our self-images become our golden idols. We justify spending money to buy clothing, cars, and status symbols that project our desired identity even as we insist that we can spare only a few dollars for the hungry and the homeless. We seek to control others and bend them to our will, and we allow ourselves to be tempted by rewards and intimidated by threats. We set up an economy of profit as a false god that cannot be questioned, and with the people of all nations and languages we bow down and serve it. Or we act as if God exists to serve us and spare us from suffering, idolizing a god who is always on our side and who exalts us above others. Yet in the midst of our idolatry, the true God is always there, smashing our inadequate images and pointing us toward the divine reality of love and justice that we perceive only in glimpses, in visions and in dreams, out of the corner of our spirits.

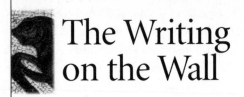

CHAPTER FOUR

The Writing on the Wall

The next three chapters of Daniel contain fabulous tales that have offered inspiration to artists through the centuries, such as Daniel surrounded by lions in their den, Nebuchadnezzar eating grass like an ox of the field, and the fantastic opulence of Belshazzar's feast as a mysterious hand writes upon the wall. Although all these stories emphasize Daniel's extraordinary wisdom, their primary focus is not Daniel but God. A refrain that runs through the chapters captures their central theme: God "is sovereign over the kingdom of mortals; he gives it to whom he will" (4:17). Each of the kings—Nebuchadnezzar, Belshazzar, and Darius—tries to claim supreme authority for himself, only to learn that the Most High is the one true sovereign. The kingdom, the power, and the glory belong to God alone.

As we discussed in chapter 2, the tales in the first half of Daniel share a common structure: a hero faces a crisis involving a king, confronts the king despite the possibly deadly consequences and, with the help of God, safely overcomes the challenge. The repeated structure builds expectation and reinforces the theological point that God, not the king, is in control of history. The pattern itself is more important than the individual identity of the hero. Daniel stars in each of the final three stories, but he is presented less as a real, flesh-and-blood person than as a figurative incarnation of justice. He embodies resistance to those who impoverish the common people in order to increase their own wealth and power. Like Robin Hood or Zorro, he is a legendary hero who personifies the critique of an unjust system, exposing the arrogance of the mighty and bringing greedy nobles to justice.

Like the legends of Robin Hood's prowess with a bow and Zorro's skill with a sword and whip, the hero tales in Daniel also have a fantastic element. Strolls in the fiery furnace, peaceable lions, and disembodied hands writing on walls make the stories both entertaining and memorable. But for people suffering under the brutality of Antiochus IV Epiphanes, such fabulous details have a more important function: they make resistance conceivable. Tyrants maintain control by terrifying people into accepting their subject state. When Moses told the Israelites that God was going to lead them out of Egypt into freedom, they initially refused to listen "because of their broken spirit and their cruel slavery" (Exodus 6:9). The promise of freedom was inconceivable until, through Moses, God showed them what divine power could accomplish. Like the staff that turns into a snake in Moses' hand, the stories in Daniel fire the imagination and inspire the Jews' will to resist the tyrant. If a mighty ruler like Nebuchadnezzar can be reduced to eating grass like an ox, then perhaps even ruthless King Antiochus is not all-powerful. If God can give Daniel the wisdom and courage he needs in times of crisis, if God is with Daniel even in the lions' den, then perhaps God will raise up leaders to confront a new challenge. When people begin to imagine defying the king, they are already halfway to taking action. The first step to freedom is believing that the tyrant is not almighty and that God alone is sovereign, a claim with serious political implications.

Although all the stories in the first half of Daniel stress the basic point that God is the one Lord to whom humans owe ultimate allegiance, they develop the theme in different ways. As we have seen, the first three chapters portray God as the giver on whom our lives depend and challenge us to recognize the false images that we worship instead of God. The stories in Daniel 4 and 5 move beyond these theological assertions and show God's power to judge kings. As punishment for his pride, Nebuchadnezzar goes mad. Because Belshazzar commits sacrilege by defiling the sacred temple vessels, he is killed and the Medes receive his kingdom. Chapter 6 mocks royal arrogance and blindness: irrevocably bound by his own foolish law, Darius is obliged to consign his favorite adviser to the lions' den. Together these last three chapters of Daniel highlight the purpose of earthly sovereignty, the limits of royal privilege, and the ways that—for good or for ill—scribes influence the behavior of kings.

Chapter 4 begins with a formal proclamation from King Nebuchadnezzar to "all peoples, nations, and languages that live throughout the earth" (4:1). As was customary among Mesopotamian kings, he speaks as if he rules the whole world. The effect is startling because Nebuchadnezzar uses the first person, directly addressing us as readers and thereby implicitly including us among his subjects. The king announces that he is going to recount "the signs and wonders that the Most High God has worked for me" (4:2). Since he is about to tell a tale of divine judgment, his claim that God's acts were on his behalf may seem surprising. Perhaps he has learned that God judges not merely to destroy, but to prepare the way for deeper, truer life.

Nebuchadnezzar begins to speak: "I, Nebuchadnezzar, was living at ease in my home and prospering in my palace. I saw a dream that frightened me; my fantasies in bed and the visions of my head terrified me" (4:4–5). The word translated as "prospering" might more accurately be translated as "flourishing," since it is frequently associated with the luxuriant growth of plants, and plant imagery plays a central role in this chapter. The king is flourishing like a plant at the height of the growing season, winning the competition for nutrients and sunlight until his life of ease is disrupted by inexplicable fear. As before, Nebuchadnezzar summons all the magicians and enchanters to help him understand what he has seen. At last Daniel arrives, identified by the king as "he who was named Belteshazzar after the name of my god and who is endowed with a spirit of the holy gods" (4:8). This time Nebuchadnezzar tells Daniel the story. In his dream he sees an immense tree planted at the center of the earth, and, like the tower of Babel in Genesis, its top reaches to heaven. In the king's telling, the tree "provided food for all. The animals of the field found shade under it, the birds of the air nested in its branches, and from it all living beings were fed" (4:12).

As the king continues to look, however, a "holy watcher" orders that the tree be cut down so that only its stump and roots remain in the ground, bound with a band of iron and bronze. "Watchers" appear in several books written around the same time as Daniel. According to the *Book of Jubilees*, they are responsible for teaching and judging human beings (Jubilees 4:15–16), while in other passages, such as 1 Enoch 15:3–12, they are fallen angels. As often happens in dreams, after the tree is cut down, the imagery suddenly and inexplicably shifts. The watcher commands that the stump be transformed from a tree into a creature that lives among the animals of the field, and that its human mind be taken from it. As one commentator observes, "The tree that provided for other living things becomes an animal that needs to be provided for, and that needy animal turns out to be a human being."[6] The watcher declares that this judgment has been rendered "in order that all who live may know that the Most High is sovereign over the kingdom of mortals; he gives it to whom he will and sets over it the lowliest of human beings" (4:17b).

> "The Most High is sovereign over the kingdom of mortals; he gives it to whom he will and sets over it the lowliest of human beings" (4:17b).

After describing the dream, Nebuchadnezzar again asks Daniel to interpret it. At this point the story reverts from Nebuchadnezzar's first-person account to the third person, so that greater emphasis falls on Daniel's words and the narrator's description. When Daniel hears the content of the dream, he is terrified and, at least at first, unwilling to speak. Nebuchadnezzar is an unpredictable and dangerous tyrant, so how can Daniel deliver a message of judgment against him? Only after the king reassures him does he open his mouth, and even then he is careful to use the language of a courtier: "'My lord, may the dream be for those who hate you, and its interpretation for your enemies!'" (4:19b). This is an extraordinarily adroit choice of words, for Daniel's statement can be understood in more than one way. Although Nebuchadnezzar no doubt thinks that Daniel is wishing judgment on his enemies, we as readers may well hear another possibility. Who hates Nebuchadnezzar more than the peoples he has conquered? The king's nightmare is their daydream.

Daniel now proceeds to interpret the dream, refocusing the vision by describing the tree in a subtly different way. Although Nebuchadnezzar sees it as a magnificent, cosmic tree that stands at the center of the earth, for Daniel it is no such thing. While Nebuchadnezzar says that the animals found shade under the tree, Daniel has them merely living under it. The NRSV translation obscures another important difference by translating the words that appear in both Daniel 4:12 and 4:21 as "provided food for all," although the Aramaic text literally states, "food for all was in it." Daniel acknowledges that "food for all was in it" (4:21) but omits the king's claim that "from it all living beings were fed" (4:12). These seemingly minor changes add up to a significantly different portrait of the tree—the king sees only the tree's splendor, while Daniel sees its failed potential. It could provide shade and food for all, but it does not do so.

> *Nebuchadnezzar's dream draws on imagery that would have been familiar to Daniel's first readers from Mesopotamian traditions as well as from the Hebrew prophets.*

Nebuchadnezzar's dream draws on imagery that would have been familiar to Daniel's first readers from Mesopotamian traditions as well as from the Hebrew prophets. In Sumerian and Assyrian literature, the king is described as a cosmic tree providing shade and sustenance for all in his kingdom, and inscriptions from Babylon and other ancient Near Eastern nations associate trees with kingship. An especially striking parallel to Nebuchadnezzar's dream appears in the prophecy of Ezekiel, which compares Pharaoh king of Egypt to a great tree planted in the garden of God. Like the tree that Nebuchadnezzar saw, this tree was a source of food and shelter, but God struck it down "because it towered high and set its top among the clouds, and its heart was proud of its height" (Ezekiel 31:10). The tree is utterly destroyed and sent down to Sheol, the abode of the dead, as an example of God's judgment on the arrogant.

Like Ezekiel, Daniel pronounces God's judgment on arrogance— the tree is Nebuchadnezzar himself. He has become extraordinarily powerful and great, but he is about to be stripped of his power and driven away from human society to live in the fields "with the mind of an animal," eating grass like an ox. He will not be returned to his throne until he has learned an essential lesson: "Heaven is sovereign" (4:26). Daniel's interpretation focuses not only on the king's pride but on his failure to care for his subjects. His kingdom has sufficient resources to sustain all who live in it, but having the resources is not the same as providing them to those in need.

Daniel recognizes that the powerful depend on the poor who live under their shadow, but when rulers and governments act unjustly, they are like trees that block the sunlight so that nothing that lives under them can grow. Scripture has taught him that human beings are not objects to be ignored or destroyed according to the royal whim, and that kings exist not to enrich themselves at the expense of their subjects, but to establish just societies and ensure that all the inhabitants of their kingdom share in its prosperity. Echoing the vision of Psalm 72, where the king is the protector of the weak and the needy, Daniel calls on Nebuchadnezzar to let God's light change the position of his shadow, so that the great tree offers shelter and shade instead of starving out the poor as if they were merely competitors for sunlight. He urges Nebuchadnezzar to repent and change his ways: "Atone for your sins with righteousness, and your iniquities with mercy to the oppressed, so that your prosperity may be prolonged" (4:27). The words are spoken to Nebuchadnezzar, but the message is directed to every king and noble.

But Daniel's call to repentance falls on deaf ears, and twelve months later Nebuchadnezzar is walking on the roof of his palace, contemplating his own greatness. "Is this not magnificent Babylon," he asks himself, "which I have built as a royal capital by my mighty power and for my glorious majesty?" (4:30). He sees everything as his own achievement, recognizing neither the God who rules over every human sovereign nor the human cost of his building program. He has no thought to spare for the conquered peoples from whom he has forcibly taken the materials to build the city. He is blind to the laborers who dug foundations, who mixed mortar, who carried tiles, who laid stone upon stone, who carved and painted the intricate art that decorated his magnificent capital. Although he did none of the actual work, he prides himself on the splendor of his accomplishment. He has no praise to spare for God because he is too busy praising his own majesty.

"While the words were still in the king's mouth," a voice from heaven announces that the judgment that Daniel predicted has fallen. Nebuchadnezzar's kingdom has been taken away, and he has been stripped not only of every royal luxury, but even of human reason. While "seven times" pass over him, he will live among the animals of the field, eating grass like an ox, reduced to the same status as the living beings that sought shade under the tree but found none. And so it comes to pass. The brutal conqueror becomes a mindless brute with hair "as long as eagles' feathers and his nails . . . like birds' claws" (4:31–33).

Ironically, the king's transformation into an animal state gives him the chance to learn what it means to be human. He has prided himself on his self-sufficiency, viewing himself as the magnificent tree from whom others derive what they need to live, so his life among the beasts teaches him that he is neither self-made nor the source of life for others. He is dependent on God for the grass he eats, for the water he drinks, for the sun that warms him, indeed, for his very life. When his sanity returns, the king speaks again in the first person and blesses the Most High for his power: "All the inhabitants of the earth are accounted as nothing, and he does what he wills with the host of heaven and the inhabitants of the earth" (4:35).

Though Nebuchadnezzar's words suggest that he has learned his lesson, the end of the story leaves us in doubt that his repentance is either genuine or lasting. He remains fascinated by his own greatness: "My majesty and splendor were restored to me for the glory of my kingdom. My counselors and my lords sought me out, . . . and still more greatness was added to me" (4:36). He expresses no interest whatsoever in the plight of his subjects. He acknowledges God's eternal sovereignty, it is true, but his praise appears to be little more than lip service. Nevertheless, his final words encapsulate one of Daniel's central themes: "Now I, Nebuchadnezzar, praise and extol and honor the King of heaven, for all his works are truth, and his ways are justice; and he is able to bring low those who walk in pride" (4:37). The contrast between the earthly and heavenly king could hardly be more obvious.

The critique of Nebuchadnezzar's kingdom would have resonated loudly in the time of Daniel's first readers. They too lived in the era

Like the biblical Daniel, the scribes who served in the court of Antiochus IV Epiphanes and who worked for the Jewish nobles who collaborated with him had hard choices to make.

of a king who cared far more about enriching himself than about providing for his subjects. Their taxes paid for his building projects, their farms and flocks provided food and materials for the royal household, but they received very little in return. Like the biblical Daniel, the scribes who served in the court of Antiochus IV Epiphanes and who worked for the Jewish nobles who collaborated with him had hard choices to make. They could remain silent in the face of oppression, protecting their own lives at the expense of the poor. They could join the resistance movement and take up arms against the king. Or they could reject both silence and violence, and taking Daniel as a mirror and a model, denounce injustice when they saw it, no matter what such faithfulness might cost them. Like Daniel, they had to decide to which sovereign they owed their deepest loyalty.

Belshazzar's Feast

Reflections on the clash between divine and human power continue in chapter 5 with the tale of Belshazzar's feast, another story of divine judgment. This time it is Belshazzar who defies God and suffers the consequences. He throws a great feast for a thousand of his lords, and under the influence of wine he calls for the gold and silver vessels that Nebuchadnezzar took from the Jerusalem temple. Accompanied by his lords and wives and concubines, he proceeds to drink wine out of the sacred vessels from the house of God while toasting his own gods "of gold and silver, bronze, iron, wood, and stone" (5:4).

"King Belshazzar" is not to be confused with Belteshazzar, Nebuchadnezzar's name for Daniel. According to the historical record, Belshazzar was the son of Nabonidus, the last king of Babylon, and although he acted as regent in his father's place, he was never officially crowned as king. The narrator, however, describes Belshazzar as the son of Nebuchadnezzar, using the terms "father" or "son" to describe their relationship no fewer than six times in this chapter. This is not necessarily an historical error, for the Hebrew Bible frequently uses the phrase "David his father" or David your father" in contexts where David is the ancestor and not the father of the king in question. An especially striking example occurs in 2 Kings 14:3:

"[Amaziah] did what was right in the sight of the LORD, yet not like his ancestor [*abiw*] David; in all things he did as his father [*abiw*] Joash had done." The Hebrew text uses the same term to refer to David and to Joash, so one might translate the verse "yet not like his father David; in all things he did as his father Joash had done." In this passage, as in many places in 1 and 2 Kings, "father" David is a standard against whom later kings are measured. The references to Belshazzar's "father" Nebuchadnezzar function in a similar way.

The story of Belshazzar's feast contrasts a powerful king with a weak one. Nebuchadnezzar conquers nations and establishes a kingdom; Belshazzar merely inherits a throne. The father inspires fear; the son buys loyalty with gifts. The father makes a monumental statue and compels his subjects to worship it; the son throws a lavish party at which he himself is the center of attention. The father has achievements to commemorate. Has the son accomplished anything significant? "His father" Nebuchadnezzar has set the bar high, and Belshazzar finds himself hopelessly unable to compete.

At his feast in front of a thousand, Belshazzar calls for "the vessels of gold and silver that his father Nebuchadnezzar had taken out of the temple in Jerusalem" (5:2). The Babylonians carried away other nations' gods to the temples of their own gods to symbolize that the Babylonian gods had defeated and imprisoned the other nations' gods. Since the Jews made no images of their God, Nebuchadnezzar had substituted the temple vessels. For Jews, the temple vessels are sacred not because they are gold and silver or because they come from Jerusalem, but because they have been made holy by proximity to God's presence. Nebuchadnezzar's removal of the vessels and Belshazzar's contemptuous abuse of them in defiance of his father have robbed the people of the rituals that allow them to approach that divine presence and appeal to God for deliverance from the depredations of tyrants. The first readers of Daniel would have recognized the similarities with their own situation. After returning from a failed attack on Egypt, Antiochus IV Epiphanes also plundered the temple treasury, removing the sacred vessels along with every gold or silver object that he could find (1 Maccabees 1:20–23). Later he desecrated the Jerusalem temple. In such a context, the story of Belshazzar's feast demonstrates that God hears the prayers of the needy even when they have no temple from which to pray and no sacred vessels to use in their religious rituals.

Belshazzar is not content merely to commit sacrilege, but tries to aggrandize himself even further by making light of his father's accomplishments and his father's religion. By taking the vessels from the temple in Jerusalem and placing them in the Babylonian temple treasury, Nebuchadnezzar has rededicated them to his own gods. When Belshazzar drinks from vessels sacred to his father's god, he is making the same kind of claim that Solomon's son Rehoboam did: "My little finger is thicker than my father's loins" (1 Kings 12:10). Belshazzar's bravado is short-lived, however, for no sooner have he and his companions begun to drink wine from the sacred vessels then the fingers of a mysterious human hand appear, writing words on the palace wall.

The king's reaction to the sight leaves no doubt that behind the swagger lies a weakling. His thoughts terrify him, just as the vision of the tree had terrified Nebuchadnezzar, but his response to fear is more dramatic: his face turns pale, "his limbs gave way, and his knees knocked together" (5:6b). The Aramaic phrase behind "his limbs gave way" can mean either that his legs collapse under him or that he loses control of his bowels. Quaking in fear at the sight before him, Belshazzar screams for his wise men, desperately offering expensive gifts and the rank of third in his kingdom to anyone who can read and interpret the writing.

Evidently Belshazzar's panic attack is noisy, for the queen hears the din from elsewhere in the palace and comes into the banquet hall to deal with the situation. She is not the queen consort, Belshazzar's wife, but the queen mother, who immediately advises him to calm down and take a page out of his father's book by consulting Daniel, who "in the days of your father . . . was found to have enlightenment, understanding, and wisdom like the wisdom of the gods" (5:11). The queen mother knows what it is important to remember, and unlike her son, she keeps her head in a crisis.

Belshazzar takes his mother's advice and summons Daniel. First he reminds him of his captive status as one of the exiles of Judah, then he flatters him, and finally he offers to reward him handsomely if he can read and interpret the writing. Daniel's response is dramatic and decisive: "Let your gifts be for yourself" (5:17). He will read and interpret the writing, but not for pay. Before he does so, however, Daniel reminds Belshazzar of the history that he ought to know but has chosen to forget. Nebuchadnezzar his father was a great king, but only because the Most High God gave him greatness. Like other Mesopotamian kings, "he killed those he wanted to kill, kept alive those he want to keep alive, honored those he wanted to honor, and degraded those he wanted to degrade." But when he overreached, claiming for himself rights that belong to God alone, God humiliated the arrogant king by reducing him to an animal state "until he learned that the Most High God has sovereignty over the kingdom of mortals, and sets over it whomever he will" (5:19b–21b).

When Daniel speaks to Belshezzar, he shows no fear and pulls no punches. Not only does the son not measure up to his father's greatness, but he has not learned from his father's mistakes. With far less reason for pride than his father, Belshazzar has exalted himself against the one true sovereign and, furthermore, he has committed sacrilege by drinking wine from God's temple vessels while praising senseless, mindless gods made of precious metals, wood, and stone. Daniel denounces Belshazzar as a fool indeed, for "the God in whose power is your very breath, and to whom belong all your ways, you have not honored" (5:23). God has not given Belshazzar greatness to equal his father's, but God does have a few words for him: MENE, MENE, TEKEL, and PARSIN.

These four words are Aramaic terms for coins and weights. The Aramaic "mene" is worth sixty shekels. A "tekel" is the Aramaic word for what is known in Hebrew as a shekel, and "parsin" means half-pieces. Daniel's interpretation of the handwriting on the wall involves some wordplay. He reinterprets the nouns as verbs derived from the same word roots, so that they mean "counted, weighed, divided"—"the obsessions of the empire (power and monetary gain, tribute payments and accounting) become the symbolic basis for judgment."[7] Using the language of economics and taxation, Daniel pronounces God's judgment on Belshazzar. The days of his kingdom are numbered. God has weighed him in the balance and found

Using the language of economics and taxation, Daniel pronounces God's judgment on Belshazzar. The days of his kingdom are numbered. God has weighed him in the balance and found him wanting.

him wanting. His kingdom will be divided and given to the Medes and Persians. Not coincidentally, the word "peres" sounds like Persians, one-half of the Medo-Persian empire that conquered Babylon.

No doubt the first readers of Daniel would have heard in this story a reference not merely to Belshazzar, but to their current king. Antiochus IV Epiphanes raided the temple treasury only a few years before the book of Daniel was written. With utter disregard for any god but himself, he used the sacred vessels and the gold taken from the temple to pay his debts and line his own pockets. He awarded the office of high priest not to the most qualified candidate, but to the one who offered him the most money. He measured his world with gold. For his Jewish subjects, the handwriting on the wall communicates a clear message: Antiochus, too, has been weighed and found wanting. Judgment is about to fall.

On the very same night that Belshazzar threw the feast and saw the handwriting on the wall, he was killed and his kingdom collapsed. According to both Herodotus and Xenophon (two ancient historians who describe Babylon's defeat), the Medes and Persians attacked Babylon during a great banquet. Xenophon reports that the people of the city were so focused on feasting and drinking that the invading army was able to dig a trench, divert the Euphrates river, and enter Babylon via the riverbed without anyone in the city raising an alarm. What an ironic end for "mighty Babylon"! With the story of Babylon's fall, the book of Daniel drives home a theological point: "the Most High God has sovereignty over the kingdom of mortals, and sets over it whomever he will." Belshazzar died unrepentant, and "Darius the Mede received the kingdom" (5:21, 31).

As far as historians have been able to determine, "Darius the Mede" is not a historical figure. It was the Persian King Cyrus the Great who, in 539 BCE, entered the city and ended the reign of Belshazzar's father Nabonidus. The Medes formed part of the Persian empire, but Cyrus was not a Mede. Furthermore, the first king known as Darius did not come to the throne until 522 BCE, after the assassination of Cyrus' son Cambyses. Darius I was not a Mede, either, but a Persian, a brilliant military commander and skilled organizer who divided the empire into administrative units known as satrapies. Apparently the biblical "Darius the Mede" is a composite character derived from the historical memories of a people for whom the identities of individual tyrants mattered less than the patterns of their cruel and oppressive behavior.

The Lions' Den

Although those who preserved the stories about Daniel may not have remembered exactly who did what in the period following the fall of Babylon, they certainly remembered the bureaucratic nature of the empire. According to Daniel 6:1, Darius establishes an elaborate administrative system overseen by 120 satraps. Evidently the new king does not find it necessary to replace all of his predecessor's advisors, since he appoints Daniel as one of the three presidents who supervise them. Daniel continues to excel as he has from his first appearance in the story, and so the king plans to promote him to first place in the kingdom.

The story of petty competition and professional jealousy that follows may well reflect the insider knowledge of the scribes who wrote the book of Daniel. As literate professionals trained to be courtiers, they would have held the same kinds of roles as the bureaucrats described in this chapter. Like the presidents and satraps, they were skilled administrators whose lives and livelihoods depended on their ability to win the king's favor. They would have been intimately familiar with the plotting and back-stabbing typical of officials seeking to secure their own positions of power. As Torah-observant Jews in a Gentile world, they knew all too well how their cultural and religious practices set them apart from the larger society. Like Daniel, they were easily identifiable as different. Their insistence on worshipping only one God, the God of Israel, made them vulnerable to the charge that they were dangerously strange, a threat to the good order of the society. The traditional stories of Daniel that the scribes have received from others and reshaped for their own day reflect the challenges that they experience in their daily lives and work.

Threatened by Daniel's success, his fellow bureaucrats look for an excuse to lay some charge against him. Despite their best efforts, however, they can find no grounds for an accusation. He is utterly faithful and responsible. He does not take bribes or participate in any of the forms of corruption endemic in most bureaucracies. In short, he is frustratingly upright, the kind of competitor whom it is very hard to defeat. He is vulnerable in one area, and one area only: his devotion to the law of his God.

At last Daniel's rivals settle on a plan. Claiming that "all the presidents of the kingdom, the prefects and the straps, the counselors and the governors" have agreed to their proposal (6:7), they persuade Darius to promulgate a new law: for thirty days any person who prays to anyone except Darius will be thrown into a pit filled with lions. Of course they are lying, for at least one president has not agreed to any such thing. But the king is easily convinced. Their suggestion appeals to his ego; the power to govern may be divided among his many subordinates, but the proposed law will make him, at least for a time, the sole granter of petitions throughout his realm. In effect, he will be granting himself divine status, as Antiochus IV Epiphanes did in the time of Daniel's first readers. Unfortunately for Darius, in his eagerness to direct toward himself the prayers that properly belong to God, he overlooks one minor but very significant detail. He is bound by his own edict, for "the law of the Medes and the Persians . . . cannot be revoked" (6:8).

The new law takes effect, and although Daniel knows about it, he persists in his regular practice of praising and praying to God three times a day. He is accustomed to praying in a room with windows open toward Jerusalem, and he continues to kneel down and pray there, in open defiance of the new edict. The envious conspirators know exactly where to find him and what to expect; as one commentator aptly puts it, "Daniel is caught acting normally."[8] Thus the satraps and presidents have framed the situation to trap Daniel between the law of his God and the law of the king. Praying to the king would, of course, be a violation of God's law. On the other hand, although thrice-daily prayer to God became customary later on, in the rabbinic period, there is nothing in the Torah that would require Daniel to pray in this way. But the narrator's portrait of Daniel indicates that prayer is an essential part of Daniel's daily life.

The satraps and presidents have framed the situation to trap Daniel between the law of his God and the law of the king.

Daniel's worship of God, his loyalty and trust, take the form not only of verbal prayer but of prayer embodied in his daily decisions and actions.

It was his deep sense of God's presence that gave him the courage to confront King Belshazzar by saying to him, "You have praised the gods of silver and gold, of bronze, iron, wood, and stone, which do not see or hear or know; but the God in whose power is your very breath, and to whom belong all your ways, you have not honored" (5:23b). In daily prayer Daniel acknowledges the basic reality that he lives under God's mercy, that in God he lives and moves and has his being. Conversely, daily worship gives him the heartfelt knowledge of God's sovereign presence that enables him to practice civil disobedience when he is confronted with injustice. He continues to pray because an unjust law cannot override God's invitation: "You speak in my heart and say, 'Seek my face.' Your face, LORD, will I seek" (Psalm 27:11).

Because seeking God's face is a regular aspect of Daniel's daily life, the conspirators find it easy to catch him in the act. At last they have the desired "ground for complaint against this Daniel." Armed with the evidence of Daniel's defiance, they crowd in to see the king. As if they were not certain, they ask the king, Didn't you sign a law that prohibits people from praying to anyone but you? Aren't violators of the law doomed to become lunch for lions? When the king replies that yes, that is the law, and it cannot be revoked, they spring the trap: "Daniel, one of the exiles from Judah, pays no attention to you, O king, or to the interdict you have signed, but he is saying his prayers three times a day" (6:13).

The wording of their accusation is important. First, they call attention to Daniel's identity as one of the exiles from Judah. Second, they accuse him of paying no heed to the king. And finally, they charge him with disobeying the new law. Like Shadrach, Meshach, and Abednego, Daniel stands out from the rest of the society because he is a Jew and the very fact of his otherness can be taken as a threat to the civic order. His story and the story of the young men in the fiery furnace encapsulate the experience of a minority group opposed to a dominant culture. Their cultural and religious distinctiveness sets them apart. Like those who denounced the three young men to Nebuchadnezzar, Daniel's accusers frame his civil disobedience not just as protest against a single law, but as direct defiance of the king. Darius knows better, as his distressed determination to save his most trusted advisor shows, but he can find no way to defend him against the charges. The rivals for Daniel's position remind Darius yet again that the laws of the Medes and Persians cannot be changed, and he capitulates—the powerful king is helpless before his own law.

At the king's command, Daniel is thrown into the lions' den. Then Darius says something surprising: "May your God, whom you faithfully serve, deliver you!" (6:16). His words are an indirect prayer, but they are a prayer nonetheless. Strictly speaking, they are a violation of the very law under which Daniel stands condemned. Darius' advisors have played to his ego by devising a law that makes him the sole granter of petitions in his realm, but ironically, if he wants his own petition granted, he must look beyond himself.

The mouth of the lions' den is shut with a stone, and then Darius seals it with his own signet and the signets of his lords, "so that nothing might be changed concerning Daniel" (6:17). Is he trying to make sure that no one will help Daniel, or that no one except the lions will hurt him? The narrator does not say, but the words add to the portrait of the king as a ruler bound by an inflexible system. Powerless to save Daniel, he spends the night sleepless and fasting. At daybreak, too worried to bother with the dignity expected of a monarch, he hurries to the lions' den and calls out through the sealed stone, "O Daniel, servant of the living God, has your God whom you faithfully serve been able to deliver you from the lions?" (6:20). A remark that on Nebuchadnezzar's lips would have been a taunt (cf. 3:15) is from Darius an expression of hope against hope. Is it possible that Daniel has escaped death?

At daybreak Darius hurries to the lions' den and calls out through the sealed stone, "O Daniel, servant of the living God, has your God whom you faithfully serve been able to deliver you from the lions?"

From the depths of the pit Daniel greets the king, announcing that God has sent an angel to shut the lions' mouths so that they would not hurt him. He has been rescued, he tells Darius, because his God has found him innocent; not only is he blameless before his God, but he has done no wrong to the king. Daniel's Hebrew name means "God is my judge," and his words make it clear that although he was condemned by the law of the Medes and Persians, his case has been heard in a higher court. The delighted king accepts the ruling and commands that Daniel be brought out of the pit. Upon inspection, "no kind of harm was found on him, because he had trusted in his God" (6:23). The word that NRSV translates as "harm" here is the same word that it translated as "wrong" in v. 22 when Daniel says, "and also before you, O king, I have done no wrong." He has neither caused harm nor received it, and so "no kind of harm was found on him." The supreme judge has pronounced a verdict, and that judgment will stand.

In an ironic reversal, judgment now falls on Daniel's accusers. The Aramaic phrase that NRSV translates as "those who had accused Daniel" could also be translated "those who had eaten the pieces of Daniel" (6:24), a figure of speech that vividly communicates both the destructive effects of slander and its cannibalistic character. At the king's command, all of the conspirators, together with their wives and children, are thrown into the lions' den. Before they even reach the bottom, they are overpowered and eaten.

Their fate, horrible though it is, provides a certain poetic justice. It resembles a passage from a psalm that we recite in church from time to time. "Happy shall they be who pay you back what you have done to us! Happy shall they be who take your little ones and dash them against the rock!" (Psalm 137:8–9). Psalm 137 was a response to Nebuchadnezzar's conquest of Jerusalem, and Daniel was written at a time when the Jews were suffering persecution under Antiochus IV Epiphanes, so in both cases God's people were seeing innocent children killed before their eyes. For the first readers of Daniel, the retributive justice of the punishment inflicted on Daniel's accusers is obvious. Nor is this longing for vengeance limited to the distant past, as should be readily apparent to anyone who remembers the national mood in the wake of the terrorist attacks on September 11, 2001. The desire for revenge is not pretty, but it is deeply human.

Nevertheless, the scene in the lions' den could be described as overkill. Because the accusers' wives and children are also thrown into the pit, this revenge is not merely an eye for an eye. No one has threatened Daniel's wife or children—as a matter of fact, we are not even told whether Daniel has a

The punishment effectively communicates two points: the brutality of the empire and its king, and the fact that in a violent system the innocent, especially the children, often suffer because of decisions in which they had no part.

wife or children. Still, the story effectively communicates two points: the brutality of the empire and its king, and the fact that in a violent system the innocent, especially the children, often suffer because of decisions in which they had no part.

At the end of chapter 6 Darius issues a decree throughout the world, commanding people throughout his dominion to "tremble and fear before the god of Daniel." Although Darius is depicted more favorably than any other king in Daniel, he still falls short of understanding the God whom Daniel worships, for Daniel's God inspires love and fidelity as well as fear and trembling. Despite the inadequacy of his theology, however, the king has learned some essential points about God's character. He praises God for doing signs and wonders and for saving Daniel, and he declares that Daniel's God is the living God whose kingdom will have no end.

Darius' decree concludes not only the story of the lions' den, but also the first major section of Daniel. With his words and the narrator's note that Daniel continues to prosper during the reigns of Darius and of Cyrus the Persian, the stories about Daniel's and his friends' lives in the royal court come to an end. As we discussed in the introduction, the court tales in these first six chapters of Daniel had been told and retold for generations. They reflect the experiences of Jews living under a variety of challenging circumstances, caught between the demands of a changing succession of imperial cultures and their commitment to God. In their present form, they present Daniel and his friends as models for faithful living in the time of Antiochus IV Epiphanes, when obeying God rather than the king was often a choice between life and death.

Like the book's first readers, Daniel and his friends are servants of God living in the realm of an earthly king, making daily decisions about whether and how they can serve two different masters. They are not perfect characters. Daniel, in particular, is fallible, falling prey at times to the same kinds of proud and self-serving behaviors that he criticizes in the kings he serves. The narrator of Daniel shapes the stories about Daniel and his friends so that the collection reflects not simply ideal behavior, but some of the less-than-perfect choices that real people in such positions actually make. They become figures for the community of God's people seeking to serve God in the real world, and their experiences reflect the challenges and temptations confronting the community of scribes among whom and for whom the book was written.

Like minorities throughout history, Daniel and his friends do not live by the norms of the society around them. Their distinctive cultural and religious practices make them vulnerable to false charges of sedition.

Like minorities throughout history, Daniel and his friends do not live by the norms of the society around them. Their distinctive cultural and religious practices make them vulnerable to charges of sedition even when they have done nothing to threaten the security of the state. Daniel's prayers and the young men's refusal to bow to the image would probably have gone unpunished if no one had reported them, but when they choose to disobey civil law because it conflicts with God's law, they are readily perceived and denounced as a threat to their society's most basic values. During the period in which these stories are set, as well as in the Hellenistic era during which they were written, preserving wealth, maintaining social status, and wielding power were among the values that the shapers of culture held most dear. Persian and Greek kings and nobles jockeyed for power and schemed for riches, and many members of the Jewish nobility collaborated.

Like Daniel and his friends, the scribes in the time of Antiochus IV Epiphanes were caught between their faith and the values of the dominant culture, tested by both privilege and suffering. As advisors to kings, nobles, and the wealthy class, they risked being seduced by the perquisites of power; as the guardians of Israel's religious traditions, they risked torture and execution if they defied the king in order to practice the faith that they taught. Some choices might cost them a promotion while others might cost them their lives, and the line between faithfulness and failure was not always clear. It was obvious that they could not offer sacrifices to Zeus and still serve the God of Israel, but could they bow before a statue of the king without violating God's commandment? Their scriptures required them to eat kosher food, but could they eat the palace food when their noble employers invited them to a feast? For them, as for us, the boundary between religion and culture was often hard to discern.

Often it was equally difficult to discern their responsibility as teachers and leaders of God's people. They were employed by a noble class that included both pagans and Jews. Should they keep their faith private when it might offend their employers? Could they accept gifts and promotions without being tempted to keep silent when they should speak out? Did it count as obeying God if they taught their fellow Jews about God's call to do justice, yet ignored the rampant injustice of the system in which they served? Or were they obligated to speak prophetically, calling attention to injustice no matter where it occurred or who committed it?

The stories in Daniel reflect the difficulty and complexity of the questions that its first readers faced. They do not offer a single solution for every situation. Sometimes, as Daniel does when invited to interpret the dream about the statue, these heroes behave with all the subtlety of politic courtiers, delivering God's message, but veiling it in images and metaphors that can be interpreted in more than one way. At other times, such as when Daniel confronts Belshazzar, they directly and bluntly speak truth to power. No matter what the situation, they cannot accept as legitimate any law that requires them to disobey the God who is sovereign over every human ruler. When the command of the king conflicts with the law of God, they practice civil disobedience. They make different decisions on different occasions, but in all that they do, they are grounded in prayer.

Today prayer and action are often discussed as if they were opposites, or as if prayer were a desperate last measure. How many times have you heard someone say, "There's nothing left to do but pray"? The book of Daniel, on the other hand, makes an intimate connection between action and prayer. From the moment that Daniel asks his friends "to seek mercy from the God of heaven" (2:18), to Daniel's doxology in chapter 2, on through the portrait of Daniel "praying and seeking mercy before his God" in chapter 6, Daniel and his friends find in the eternal God the source of their wisdom and strength. They recognize that "prayer is not a pious instrument by which we move God to baptize our enterprises; it is entering the strength of him who moves history and binds the powers that be."[9] Without prayer, Daniel and his friends would merely be sages confronting foreign kings—if they could find in themselves the courage to confront them at all. With prayer, they become bearers of God's word and living reminders of God's reign. Through prayer and faith-

ful action they make visible to those who would
not otherwise perceive it the presence of the invis-
ible God.

Without prayer, Daniel and his friends would merely be sages confronting foreign kings—if they could find in themselves the courage to confront them at all. With prayer, they become bearers of God's word and living reminders of God's reign.

Time after time the prayers and confessions of
praise in the first six chapters of Daniel affirm
God's sovereignty. They declare that the world is
God's domain and that every earthly sovereign is
judged by God, who "changes times and season,
deposes kings and sets up kings" (2:21). The stories
as well as the hymns reveal the God of Israel as one
who humiliates the arrogant and lifts up the lowly. Like Hannah's
song in 1 Samuel and Mary's magnificat in Luke, they celebrate the
God who breaks the bows of the mighty and gives strength to the fee-
ble, who fills the hungry with good things and sends the rich away
empty. The book of Daniel adds its voice to the biblical proclamation
of God's love and justice, for as even the mighty king Nebuchadnezzar at last confesses, "all his works are truth, and his ways are justice;
and he is able to bring low those who walk in pride" (4:37).

Stories and hymns together proclaim a God who judges in order
to save, who destroys in order to build anew. The vision of the tree in
all its splendor is a dream not merely of judgment but of another
possible world, a world in which the earth's abundance exists not
only for the powerful, but for those who live in their shadow. When
the tree fails to provide, the watchers cut it down. Nevertheless, its
stump remains, embodying the hope that the tree may yet sprout,
flourishing and offering its fruits and shade to all.

The first six chapters of Daniel make use of court tales, prayers,
and the interpretation of dreams to portray God as the eternal sovereign who reigns in justice and truth. The last six chapters of the
book, which focus on Daniel's prayer of confession and his visions
of the future, reinforce the picture. To those chapters we now turn.

CHAPTER FIVE

The Night Visions

I, Daniel, saw in my vision by night the four winds of heaven stirring up the great sea, and four great beasts came up out of the sea, different from one another. The first was like a lion and had eagles' wings. Then, as I watched, its wings were plucked off, and it was lifted up from the ground and made to stand on two feet like a human being; and a human mind was given to it. Another beast appeared, a second one, that looked like a bear. It was raised up on one side, had three tusks in its mouth among its teeth and was told, "Arise, devour many bodies!" After this, as I watched, another appeared, like a leopard. The beast had four wings of a bird on its back and four heads; and dominion was given to it. After this I saw in the visions by night a fourth beast, terrifying and dreadful and exceedingly strong. It had great iron teeth and was devouring, breaking in pieces, and stamping what was left with its feet. It was different from all the beasts that preceded it, and it had ten horns. (7:2–7)

With this vision we have reached a turning point in the book. The first half of Daniel contains six tales that portray Daniel and his friends dealing with the challenges of living in exile as servants of kings whose despotic and arbitrary power they are often called to protest. In the series of apocalyptic visions that begins in chapter 7, however, Daniel the courtier and wise man stands face to face not with earthly kings, but with the divine realm. It is here also that the fingerprints of the scribal authors appear most clearly, as Daniel begins to narrate his own story in the first person, speaking directly to us and offering insights into his internal responses, his questions and his fears. Until this point Daniel has explained the meaning of dreams that the wisest of the king's sages could not comprehend, but from chapter 7 on he plays a different role. Now the interpreter of dreams becomes the dreamer, and the wise counselor is left struggling to make sense of mysteries that even he does not understand.

With the opening words of Daniel's vision in chapter 7, we realize that we have left dreams of golden statues and enormous trees far behind to enter a strange new world populated with bizarre animals and majestic heavenly beings. As the vision continues to unfold, Daniel sees an Ancient One seated on a throne, watches as the beasts are judged and as one like a human being receives dominion, and talks with an angel about the meaning of what he has seen. In chapter 8, Daniel has a second, equally fantastic vision: a two-horned ram defeated by a goat with a great horn that is broken off and replaced with four smaller horns. Although an angelic figure once again interprets the vision for Daniel, he remains dismayed and perplexed.

Like Daniel, the scribes who wrote the book were faced with mysteries that they could not understand. Antiochus IV Epiphanes had outlawed the religious practices that formed the basis of the Jews' identity as God's people. His blasphemous words and brutal behavior threatened to wipe out not just individual Jews, but the entire Jewish way of life. How could God allow this to happen? How long would it go on? Would they survive? Did God still care about them? As teachers and leaders of the people, the scribes turned to their sacred texts and traditions, reviewing the history of Israel as it had been passed down to them, seeking a solution to an apparently hopeless situation, trying to discern when or whether the true God, the Most High, would manifest divine power and destroy the arrogant imposter Antiochus IV Epiphanes.

The visions in Daniel 7–12, full of images drawn from Israel's scriptures, reflect the scribes' insights into Israel's past, their reflections on the meaning of the present crisis, and their hopes for the future. They express the assurance that the God who has delivered Israel from a series of unjust and exploitative empires will act again to free the people from Antiochus' brutal reign. They look to a future when the wise among the people will, like the human one who descends from the clouds, receive a kingdom and be entrusted with the responsibility of ruling justly.

Although the last half of Daniel reviews the history of Israel's life under a series of conquerors and then focuses on the crisis under Antiochus IV, it veils its message in the symbolic language of apocalyptic literature. The authors of the book lived and worked in the courts of the powerful, so writing about Antiochus was full of risk. That is why the scribes who composed Daniel used coded language, urging their peers to take a stand against the blasphemous king. Though they were writing at the beginning of the violent Maccabean revolt, they called for patient, nonviolent resistance.

> Although the last half of Daniel reviews the history of Israel under tyranny and then focuses on the crisis under Antiochus IV, it veils its message in the symbolic language of apocalyptic literature.

Historians have long recognized that most of the events presented as prophecies in Daniel's visions had already occurred by the time Daniel was written. The most detailed and exact historical descriptions are of events that took place during the authors' own lifetimes, just before and during Antiochus' reign. The historical inaccuracies that we have noted in the court stories show that the scribes who collected and edited the tales had an imperfect knowledge of the more distant events of the Babylonian and Persian periods. Nevertheless, the outline of Israel's history showed them that the present system originated in and built upon the unjust practices and patterns of empires long fallen, and taught them that God had enabled their people to survive their ongoing subjugation. It reinforced their belief that God works through human beings. The visions that the scribes attributed to Daniel offer the hope that Israel's future will be different because the people of God will resist the blasphemies of their rulers and will offer their loyalty to God alone. Furthermore, they look beyond the fall of the tyrant Antiochus and envision a just society established by the sovereign God.

The visions in Daniel 7 and 8 are set during Belshazzar's reign. Since chapter 5 describes the events leading up to Belshazzar's death and chapter 6 takes place during the reign of Darius (who, according to Daniel, conquered Belshazzar's kingdom and took his throne), the narrative has already moved past this point. At the narrative level, then, we are dealing with a series of flashbacks to earlier points in Daniel's life. By referring to an earlier time and to a king whose death it has already recounted, the book of Daniel reminds us that even the seemingly invincible Babylonian empire came to an end. To readers suffering Antiochus' reign of terror the message would have been clear: Take heart! No earthly empire lasts forever!

As chapter 7 begins, it is the first year of Belshazzar, and Daniel experiences something that he refers to repeatedly as "a night vision" or "a vision by night." His language invites symbolic interpretation, for at night the scribes moved through courts illuminated only by lamps and torches. The way forward was not always clearly visible. They passed through well-lit areas back into the darkness, where it was easy to stumble and fall. Although the shadows might hold hidden threats, they also offered advantages: nighttime and darkness allowed for quiet conversations and discreet pondering of possibilities. In his struggles to understand the night vision, Daniel represents the book's scribal authors, trying to discern a path that would lead them out of subjugation under Antiochus and into freedom. He symbolizes the sages, clustered in dark corners, considering their options as they confront a crisis that frightens and exhausts them but has not defeated them. Like the scribes, Daniel peers into a shadowy past in order to make sense of the present darkness. In the night vision he brings the scribes' questions and fears from the human courts where they live into the throne room of God.

> *Like the scribes, Daniel peers into a shadowy past in order to make sense of the present darkness. In the night vision he brings the scribes' questions and fears from the human courts where they live into the throne room of God.*

The Four Beasts and the Heavenly Court

Daniel's night vision is divided into two scenes. The first focuses on four warring, grotesque beasts and the second takes place in the divine court. Regarding the first scene Daniel writes, "I, Daniel, saw in my vision by night the four winds of heaven stirring up the great sea, and four great beasts came up out of the sea, different from one another" (7:2–3). In biblical times the four winds represented the four directions, north, south, east, and west; here they suggest the global impact of the great beasts. In Ancient Near Eastern culture, the sea was a common symbol for chaos, and some myths depicted the creation of the world as the outcome of a primeval battle between the gods and chaos monsters associated with the sea. *Yam,* the Hebrew word for sea, was also the name of one of the chaos monsters in the creation myths. Numerous passages in the Old Testament use imagery taken from this symbolic world. For example, in a passage about the creation of the world, the psalmist celebrates God's conquest of the chaotic powers: "You divided the sea by your might; you broke the heads of the dragons in the waters. You crushed the heads of Leviathan" (Psalm 74:13–14a). Daniel's vision of the sea and the beasts that rise from it draws on this symbolic language to evoke a time when God's people fear that the orderly world is dissolving into chaos.

Although the first three beasts are terrible and grotesque, Daniel's attention is fixed on the fourth beast, which breaks its prey in pieces, devouring them with iron teeth and stamping the remains with its feet. This fourth beast has ten horns, and as Daniel watches, three of its horns are plucked out to make room for a little horn with human eyes and a big mouth.

As Daniel continues to watch, the scene abruptly changes to the divine court, where chaos and destruction give way to majestic order. Daniel's speech pattern changes as well, for it shifts from prose to poetry as he begins to describe a sight utterly different from what has gone before:

> As I watched,
> thrones were set in place,
> and an Ancient One took his throne;
> his clothing was white as snow,
> and the hair of his head like pure wool;
> his throne was fiery flames,
> and its wheels were burning fire. (7:9)

The imagery of the passage—throne, garments white as snow, fire—as well as the events that soon unfold leave no doubt that the figure whom Daniel sees is God, enthroned amid the divine court. Other biblical passages such as Isaiah 6 and Psalm 97 portray God as seated on a throne and served by heavenly attendants, and the Bible repeatedly depicts God as appearing in or surrounded by fire. The closest biblical parallel to Daniel's vision is found in Ezekiel, where God, seated on a fiery, wheeled throne, commissions the prophet as a human messenger to the people of Israel.

Although Daniel's description of God as an Ancient One (literally, "Ancient of Days") appears nowhere else in the Old Testament, it echoes other biblical references to God as the one who is "enthroned forever," and "whose years endure throughout all generations" (Psalm 102:12, 24). In biblical times, describing something as "ancient" suggested not that it was worn-out or worthless, but that it was of great value. The aged were regarded with great respect as those who had the life experience to make wise judgments and offer counsel to others. At the opposite end of the spectrum from the "Ancient of Days," mortals are "few of days": "A mortal, born of woman, few of days and full of trouble, comes up like a flower and withers, flees like a shadow and does not last" (Job 14:1–2). God is the Ancient One, while human lives and human plans are as ephemeral as grass. Daniel's vision serves to emphasize a theme that has been sounded repeatedly throughout the book: human kingdoms rise and fall, but God's reign endures forever.

The Ancient One is enthroned in majesty, and as Daniel watches, the books are opened and the court case begins. The beasts of chaos come under divine judgment. The little horn with the big mouth makes arrogant noises, but evidently the words it speaks are not worth reporting. Its voice falls silent as the fourth beast is put to death and its body is burned. The other beasts are allowed to live for a time, but they no longer exercise dominion, and their power has been taken away.

Now a new character enters the stage. Daniel sees "one like a human being" (7:13). The RSV, NIV, and many other versions translate the Aramaic phrase as "one like a son of man." Either way that the words are translated, they emphasize the human appearance of this figure who comes with the clouds of heaven and is given "dominion and glory and kingship." Unlike the power of the beasts that dominated the earth only for a time, "his dominion is an everlasting dominion that shall not pass away, and his kingship is one that shall never be destroyed" (7:14). It is a startling description, since passages such as Darius' doxology at the end of chapter 6 have emphasized that eternal dominion belongs to God alone.

At this point the vision takes a surprising turn. Thus far Daniel has been an observer, watching the events unfolding as if from a distance. Now, troubled and terrified, he enters into the action of the dream, approaching one of the attendants to ask for an interpretation of what he has seen. The angelic attendant explains that the four great beasts represent four kings, "but the holy ones of the Most High shall receive the kingdom and possess the kingdom forever—forever and ever" (7:18). The attendant focuses on the holy ones who receive the kingdom, but Daniel remains fixed on

> Now, troubled and terrified, Daniel enters into the action of the dream, approaching one of the attendants to ask for an interpretation of what he has seen.

the terrifying fourth beast, its ten horns, and especially on the horn with human eyes and a mouth that speaks big words. He asks to know the truth about it, rehearsing what he has seen and mentioning details that were not present in his first account of the scene. He describes the beast's terrifying bronze claws and says that the horn with the arrogant mouth "seemed greater than the others." Then he adds a particularly significant piece of information: the horn had been making war against the holy ones, and until the Ancient One appeared, it seemed to be winning.

The angel explains that the fourth beast is a fourth kingdom different from all the others, a kingdom that devours and destroys and breaks in pieces. The ten horns stand for ten kings who will be succeeded by another king, who will displace three kings in order to make room for himself. Most significantly, "he shall speak words against the Most High, shall wear out the holy ones of the Most High, and shall attempt to change the sacred seasons and the law; and they shall be given into his power for a time, two times, and half a time" (7:25). After this period, the court will pass judgment on him, and his dominion will be "consumed and utterly destroyed."

Then "the people of the holy ones of the Most High" (7:27) will be given a kingdom that will never end, and all other dominions will serve them.

Taken together with the details that Daniel offers in his description of the beasts, the angel's explanation of the vision gives us the clues that we need to recognize the historical references. Daniel describes the first beast as like a lion, but with the wings of an eagle. This nightmarish hybrid would have seemed less grotesque to his first readers than to us, since composite creatures such as winged lions appeared in the art of many countries, including Assyria and Babylonia. In the Hebrew scriptures, eagles are associated with tremendous speed, and lions often symbolize oppressive rulers or attacking armies—"Like a roaring lion or a charging bear is a wicked ruler over a poor people" (Proverbs 28:15). The first beast in Daniel 7 is drawn from this symbolic world. Its wings are plucked off, it is made to stand upright like a human, and it receives a human mind, which recalls the story of Nebuchadnezzar's madness, when the king's mind was changed from human to animal and back again. The four beasts in Daniel's vision and the statue that Nebuchadnezzar saw in his dream symbolize the same historical succession of kingdoms. Earlier Daniel identifies the statue's head of gold as Nebuchadnezzar himself, and here the winged lion that receives a human heart symbolizes both Nebuchadnezzar and the conquering might of Babylon.

The second beast looks like a bear with something extra in its mouth, either three tusks (as NRSV has it), or three ribs, an image that brings to mind the oracle of Amos, where a shepherd rescues "two legs, or a piece of an ear" from a wild beast's mouth (3:12). The bearlike beast in Daniel, who is raised up on one side as if deformed or crippled, receives a direct command, though we are not told from whom: "Arise, devour many bodies!" (7:5). The devouring bear is the Medes, who (according to Daniel's understanding of history) attacked and defeated Babylon.

The third beast is even more grotesque: it resembles a four-headed leopard with four wings, but we are told nothing more about it except that it is given "dominion." In the Bible leopards, like bears and lions, are dangerous predators. This beast's four wings and four heads add to the ferocity of the picture, intensifying both the leopard's already notorious speed and its ability to watch and stalk its prey. It represents the Persians, who, under Cyrus the Great, were renowned for their rapid conquest of the Ancient Near East. Finally, like the feet of iron and clay in the statue that Nebuchadnezzar saw, the fourth beast with the iron teeth represents the Greek Empire, which in Daniel's time was governed by members of the Seleucid dynasty.

If other clues were not sufficient, the horns on the fourth beast also help to establish its identity. Coins from the second century BCE, when Daniel was written, depict Seleucid kings wearing horned helmets. Although the Ptolemaic and Seleucid kings who succeeded Alexander the Great can be counted in several different ways, ultimately the precise identification of the kings represented by each of the ten horns does not matter, since the overall reference is clear. The three horns uprooted by "the little horn" are easier to identify exactly: after the death of Antiochus III, three people were in line for the throne ahead of the man who became Antiochus IV Epiphanes. Two were murdered, and one became a hostage in Rome. Antiochus IV was responsible for only one of the murders, that of Antiochus, his brother's son, but it would have been clear to the first readers of Daniel that three people had been eliminated before he claimed the throne.

The angel's description of the little horn leaves no doubt whom this image represents. Like the arrogant king in the vision, Antiochus spoke "words against the Most High." He declared himself to be God manifest, even going so far as to write the claim on some of his coins. He tried to "change the sacred seasons and the law" by issuing edicts that prohibited not only the observance of the Sabbath and of the Jewish holy days, but also the practice of circumcision. Other kings in Israel's history had defeated the nation and exiled the people, had even destroyed the temple, but no other king had so directly attacked their faith. For that reason, to the Jews who were suffering under his brutal reign, he did indeed seem greater and more terrifying than all the kings who had gone before. Wise courtiers might have been able to use their well-honed political skills to navigate the dangerous courts of kings like Nebuchadnezzar and Darius without compromising their faith, but the Jewish scribes in the era of Antiochus IV had much more limited options: serve the king and his gods; practice their faith secretly and risk death if they were discovered; or confess their faith openly and be executed.

Just as the beasts symbolize a succession of kingdoms and the little horn symbolizes Antiochus IV, so the Daniel of the vision represents the scribes who had to deal with him. The Daniel that we see in the last chapters of the book takes on a complexity that was only rarely apparent earlier. His piety and wisdom are no longer the focus; now his humanity comes to the fore. Daniel is seen to be terribly aware of his human frailty and weakness. Like the scribes in Antiochus' day, he is faced with an unprecedented situation. The scribes were the bearers of the religious traditions of their people. They were the leaders who had devoted their lives to helping others make wise decisions, but now, when their wisdom was most needed, they must have felt like Daniel: helpless, confused, and afraid.

His piety and wisdom are no longer the focus; now his humanity comes to the fore. Daniel is seen to be terribly aware of his human frailty and weakness.

The scene in the heavenly court gives the scribes a way to ask questions and express their concerns, but it also gives them a vision and a hope. No matter how terrifying the fourth beast may seem, ultimately it is no match for the Ancient One and the heavenly armies. The words "a time, two times, and half a time" in Daniel 7:25 are deliberately nonspecific; although the fearsome beast may seem to have gained the upper hand for a while, its dominion will not last forever. Like every earthly ruler, it is mortal, finite, and doomed to die.

The vision draws a sharp contrast between the ferocious beasts who come from the sea and the "one like a human being" who comes on the clouds of heaven. The former are savage brutes, inhuman monsters who rise out of chaos and bring death, but the latter comes not from the chaotic waters, but from God's dwelling place. His arrival is awe-inspiring but not fearsome, majestic rather than terrifying. If the beasts are inhuman, he is humane. He does not seize a kingdom by destroying all who oppose him, but receives kingship from the Ancient One and embodies on earth the eternal reign of God. He receives dominion so that the whole world may become the domain of God, the place where God dwells. Unlike the beasts, whose power lasts only for a time, his kingdom will have no end.

If the beasts symbolize a historical series of kingdoms, and the little horn is Antiochus IV, then who is this human figure, this one like a son of man? Although the angelic attendant offers some clues to this figure's identity, the answer continues to be disputed. When Daniel first asks him for an explanation of the vision, the angel tells him, "the holy ones of the Most High shall receive the kingdom and possess the kingdom forever." He refers to the "holy ones of the Most High" again in his second, longer interpretation of the dream, and at the end of his explanation claims that kingship "shall be given to the people of the holy ones of the Most High" (7:18–27). The angel's words and the identity of the holy ones have puzzled interpreters for centuries.

A look ahead at later chapters provides some clues. For example, in chapter 8 Daniel hears one "holy one" speaking to another, and the context leaves no doubt that both are angelic figures, members of the heavenly host. Later chapters also mention the angel Gabriel, who is described as "having the appearance of a man" (8:15; cf. 9:21). The Hebrew word that is translated "man" indicates a strong man or warrior and is not the same as the word used in the phrase "one like a human being," but the text clearly emphasizes Gabriel's human appearance. Later still Daniel converses with an angelic being described as "one in human form" who tells Daniel about Michael, "one of the chief princes," whom he also describes as "your prince" (10:13, 21). Michael and Gabriel are both archangels, princes charged with protecting particular nations against opposing princes who are making war on them, and the people of Israel are Michael's special responsibility.

Because Michael has such an important role in the book, some scholars have suggested that "the one like a human being" in Daniel 7 is the archangel himself, but this conclusion ignores an important detail in the text. Since the angelic interpreter explains the vision by saying that the kingdom will be given to "the holy ones"—plural, not singular—Michael is too specific an answer. The evidence within Daniel suggests, then, that the "one like a human being" represents the whole company of angelic beings, the heavenly host. They have been worn out by their struggles against the hostile angels of other nations who make war on them, but only for a time. The day will come when God will give the kingdom into their hands.

In the book of Daniel, heavenly realities and conflicts have their mirror image on earth, and heavenly beings have earthly counterparts. The four beasts symbolize the powerful enemies of God's people, and, as we shall see later on, the archangels represent particular nations, giving visible form to their struggles, their weariness, their failures, and their triumphs. In the same way, the holy ones in heaven correspond to God's holy ones on earth; "the people of the holy ones of the Most High" are God's people, Israel. At Mt. Sinai God promised that they would be "a priestly kingdom and a holy nation" (Exodus 19:6). In his night vision Daniel sees the promise fulfilled: the reign of God is entrusted to God's people.

In his night vision Daniel sees the promise fulfilled: the reign of God is entrusted to God's people.

Although the people of the holy ones receive eternal dominion, the point is not that the Jewish people as such will become invincible. Their power and authority are derivative, given to them by God. The entire book of Daniel emphasizes the reality that human power and human beings are temporal and limited. It calls God's people to place their faith and hope moment by moment in God, the maker of all and the one true sovereign. Daniel's night vision reveals the hidden power given to believers who trust that the creator will put an end to the mighty but ultimately illusory power of the human empires that crush and oppress them. The "one like a human being" is the prototype of the fully human being, a vision of the abundant life that becomes possible for God's people when they offer themselves freely in the service of their creator.

Daniel's night vision reveals the hidden power given to believers who trust that the creator will put an end to the mighty but ultimately illusory power of the human empires that crush and oppress them.

Daniel's vision of the one like a human being (more commonly translated "one like a son of man") has captured the imagination of readers throughout the centuries. Because it sparked a new way of thinking about the relationship between God and humankind, it is among the most influential images from the Hebrew Bible. Jewish literature documents that some rabbis during the

Roman period interpreted this humanlike figure as the promised messiah, the Davidic king anointed by God. They interpreted Daniel 7 as a prophecy that the messiah would conquer Israel's enemies and that under his leadership Israel would be a free and prosperous nation that reigned over the whole earth. This line of thought both resembles and differs from Christian uses of the expression.

Most Christians know the term "Son of Man" from reading the New Testament: it is Jesus' preferred way to refer to himself in the gospels. Sometimes Jesus uses the phrase to emphasize his role as a vulnerable and suffering human being—"Foxes have holes, and birds of the air have nests; but the Son of Man has nowhere to lay his head" (Matthew 8:20)—and each time that Jesus predicts his arrest, trial, and crucifixion, he also uses this title: "Then he began to teach them that the Son of Man must undergo great suffering, and be rejected by the elders, the chief priests, and the scribes, and be killed, and after three days rise again" (Mark 8:31). On other occasions, Jesus portrays the Son of Man as a heavenly and apocalyptic figure, clearly alluding to and sometimes even directly quoting Daniel 7:13. For example, in Mark 13 he points to a future time when, after great trials and calamities, people "will see 'the Son of Man coming in clouds' with great power and glory" to "gather his elect from the four winds" (vv. 26, 27). To sum up, Jesus uses "Son of Man" to denote himself as the fully human one who shares our human weakness and who comes not to be served but to serve, who suffers and dies to ransom his people from their sins, is raised from the dead, and will return as heavenly ruler and judge. Jesus' interpretation of the term draws on Daniel but develops the image in ways that go well beyond its meaning in Daniel 7.

The book of Revelation takes the image from Daniel a step further. John sees the Son of Man in his heavenly glory, describing him in terms that echo Daniel's vision of the Ancient One: "His head and his hair were white as white wool, white as snow" (Revelation 1:14). Throughout, the emphasis falls heavily on the Son of Man as ruler and judge, and his human aspect receives little attention. Still later, in the second century, Irenaeus of Lyons took the trajectory that began in Daniel and continued in the gospels and developed it still further, interpreting the Son of Man as the ideal human being who opened the way for all people to become what God created humans to be. According to Irenaeus, God took on human form and shared in the human experience so that humans could be transformed into the divine image. Therefore the Son of Man calls people beyond their preoccupation with earthly needs and power struggles into the freedom of God's reign and the fullness of divine life. Irenaeus' use of the Son of Man image draws far more on the New Testament than on the Hebrew Scriptures, but the beginnings of the idea are already apparent in Daniel 7.

After he receives the interpretation of his vision, Daniel is left pale and shaken. He has seen a heavenly vision, but so many earthly questions remain unanswered. When will the imposter fall? When he is destroyed, what is to prevent other bestial rulers from taking his place? What role will the scribes have in these events? What responsibility do they have to God's people? At the end of the vision, Daniel remains speechless, contemplating what he has seen. The curtain falls, and the stage is set for the next scene.

The Ram and the Goat

Daniel 8 begins much as the previous chapter did, with a reference to Belshazzar's reign, and once again Daniel has a vision that is interpreted by an angel. What is surprising, however, is that the book has reverted to the language of the first chapter. From this point on to the end, Daniel is written in Hebrew, the Jewish people's own language, and not Aramaic, the language that they learned in captivity. The authors' Aramaic is much better than their Hebrew, but the decision to write in the historic language of their people may reflect their attempt to reclaim the very culture that their oppressor is trying to exterminate. Since they do not explain, we can only guess at their reasons.

"In the third year of the reign of King Belshazzar a vision appeared to me, Daniel. . . ." As the curtain rises on the next scene, Daniel sees himself by the river Ulai in Susa, the capital of the province of Elam. During Belshazzar's time in the sixth century BCE, Susa was the Babylonians' rather rundown seasonal capital, but by the second century it would have been familiar to Daniel's readers for other reasons as well. Susa was one of several royal residences during the Persian period and, significantly, it was there that Queen Esther and her uncle Mordecai thwarted Haman's plan and exacted vengeance on those who had plotted to exterminate the Jewish people. By Antiochus IV's reign, Susa on the Eulaeus (=Ulai) had been developed by the Seleucid dynasty into an exemplary Greek polis, or city-state. Daniel's first readers would have recognized it not only as the site of a famous Jewish triumph over their enemies but as a prime example of Hellenistic culture and values.

In the vision, Daniel looks up and sees a ram standing by the river, with one of its horns longer than the other. Daniel watches as the ram charges toward the west, north, and south, noting, "All beasts were powerless to withstand it, and no one could rescue from its power; it did as it pleased and became strong" (8:4b). As Daniel continues to watch, a male goat with a single horn between its eyes speeds across the whole earth from the west and attacks the ram, breaking both its horns and then trampling the ram on the ground. The mighty ram is helpless before the male goat—"there was no one who could rescue the ram from its power"—but "at the height of its power," the great horn is broken off, and in its place grow up four prominent horns that point toward the four winds. As Daniel continues to watch,

> "Out of one of them came another horn, a little one, which grew exceedingly great toward the south, toward the east, and toward the beautiful land. It grew as high as the host of heaven" (8:9–10).

> Out of one of them came another horn, a little one, which grew exceedingly great toward the south, toward the east, and toward the beautiful land. It grew as high as the host of heaven. It threw down to the earth some of the host and some of the stars, and trampled on them. Even against the prince of the host it acted arrogantly; it took the regular burnt offering away from him and overthrew the place of his sanctuary. Because of wickedness, the host was given over to it together with the regular burnt offering; it cast truth to the ground, and kept prospering in what it did. (8:9–12)

Next Daniel hears two holy ones speaking. One asks the other, "For how long is this vision concerning the regular burnt offering, the transgression that makes desolate, and the giving over of the sanctuary and host to be trampled?" (8:13b). The reply is precise: "For two thousand three hundred evenings and mornings; then the sanctuary shall be restored to its rightful state" (8:14).

Daniel has seen the vision, but he is at a loss to interpret it until a human voice calls out, "Gabriel, help this man understand the vision." As the angel approaches, Daniel falls prostrate with terror. Gabriel addresses him as "Mortal" (literally, "son of man"), lifting him to his feet and telling him that the vision is for the time of the end, of "what will take place later in the period of wrath" (8:19).

Now Gabriel begins his interpretation. Although the angel had identified the beasts in the first vision only vaguely, as four kingdoms, Gabriel is specific and exact: the ram with two horns is the kings of Media and Persia. In ancient Mesopotamian astrology, the sign of the zodiac for Persia was a ram, and like the charging ram, the Medes and Persians conquered nations to their north, west, and south. Gabriel goes on to identify the male goat who appeared from the west as the king of Greece, and its great horn as "the first king." Although he does not identify this king by name, Daniel's first readers would have recognized him immediately as Alexander the Great, the king whose armies marched eastward from Macedonia and within three years controlled the territory from Asia Minor to Persia to the border of Egypt. In Daniel's vision, the great horn is broken "at the height of its power," and indeed Alexander died young, at the age of thirty-two. The four horns that replace the great horn and point toward the four winds are four weaker kingdoms that have risen from Alexander's and are controlled by the Diadochi, the generals who fought to become Alexander's successors and who divided his empire among themselves. One of these divisions was the Seleucid empire, based in Syria, and Antiochus IV Epiphanes was a Seleucid king.

But what of the little horn that is the climax of Daniel's vision, which "grew as high as the host of heaven" and violated the sanctuary?

At the end of their rule,
   when the transgressions have reached their full measure,
a king of bold countenance shall arise,
   skilled in intrigue.
He shall grow strong in power,
   shall cause fearful destruction,
   and shall succeed in what he does.

He shall destroy the powerful
  and the people of the holy ones.
By his cunning
  he shall make deceit prosper under his hand,
  and in his own mind he shall be great.
Without warning he shall destroy many
  and shall even rise up against the Prince of princes.
But he shall be broken, and not by human hands. (8:23–25)

Although Gabriel has already described the ram as the Medes and Persians and the goat as Greece, he does not identify the little horn by name. In a dangerous situation, some things are best left unsaid. In any case, Daniel's first readers would have recognized the "king of bold countenance" as Antiochus IV Epiphanes. Despite his terrifying power, Antiochus—like the statue in Nebuchadnezzar's dream—will eventually be broken "not by human hands." His destruction will come at God's command and through divine means. So the implication for Daniel's original readers would have been clear: overthrowing Antiochus was God's task, not theirs.

The visions in Daniel 7 and 8 both end with the reign of Antiochus, but they reflect slightly different periods in his persecution of the Jews.

The visions in Daniel 7 and 8 both deal with a succession of kingdoms and end with the reign of Antiochus, but they reflect slightly different periods in his persecution of the Jews. On the fifteenth day of the Jewish month of Chislev in 167 BCE, Antiochus built an altar to Zeus over the altar of burnt offering in God's temple in Jerusalem, defiling the temple. For three years the Jews were unable to offer burnt offerings to God. Finally, on 25 Chislev 164, the temple was rededicated, and the regular burnt offerings were restored. Although Daniel 7 describes the fourth beast's terrifying violence and the little horn's arrogance, it makes no mention of the temple or the burnt offerings. It is probable, therefore, that Daniel 7 was written after 169 BCE, when Antiochus had begun his persecution of the Jews and his attempts to exterminate their culture and their religious practices, but before the desecration of the temple. Daniel 8, on the other hand, was likely written sometime between 167 and 164, since the holy one's question in Daniel 8:13 about how long the people will have to endure the trampling of the sanctuary, the giving over of the burnt offerings, and "the transgression that makes desolate" reflects knowledge of the desecration but not of the rededication.

The length of the desecration is clearly an important issue, since at the conclusion of the vision in Daniel 8, Gabriel reassures Daniel regarding the truth of what he has been told about the 2,300 evenings and mornings. Moreover, questions about time will be raised repeatedly in the remaining chapters of the book. At this point, however, Daniel is given no further information. Instead, the angel tells the seer, "Seal up the vision, for it refers to many days from now" (8:26).

Gabriel's indication that the vision concerns a time in the distant future, as well as his earlier, repeated references to "the time of the end," have led interpreters such as Hal Lindsey, Jerry Falwell, and Tim LaHaye to conclude that Daniel's vision is about the last judgment and the end of history. In their literary and historical context, however, these time references have an entirely different meaning. In the first place, from the point of view of the legendary character Daniel, whom the book portrays as having seen this vision during the third year of Belshazzar's reign in the sixth century BCE, the desecration and restoration of the temple in the second century would have been "many days from now." Furthermore, Gabriel's reference to "the period of wrath" makes perfect sense when interpreted as a description of Antiochus' reign of terror, and "the appointed time of the end" (8:19) means the end of the historical crisis with Antiochus, when the sanctuary will be cleansed, the sacrifices will be restored, and God's people will live in peace and safety.

Despite the angel's assurance that the "king of bold countenance" will be broken and that the vision of the evenings and mornings is true, Daniel is so overwhelmed by what he has seen that he spends a number of days sick in bed. Eventually he gets up and carries on with "the king's business." The end of the chapter calls attention to two issues: Daniel remains in his tenuous position, working for a doomed king; and even though Gabriel has interpreted the vision for him, he still does not understand it.

The scribes who wrote the book, as well as its first readers, must have found themselves in a position very similar to Daniel's. Entrusted with the wisdom and insight that their people needed, they also trusted in God's power to overthrow Antiochus and bring an end to persecution. Nevertheless, they did not know how or when God would act, and while they waited for divine intervention, they continued to serve the very people whom God would soon judge. In such a delicate situation, what should they do—go on working as if nothing had changed, waiting for God to act? Or prepare themselves to take action when the critical moment arrived? Should they leave their positions in the courts of the powerful? By emphasizing Daniel's reactions to the visions, chapters 7 and 8 bring such questions to the fore, and the final chapters of Daniel will pay increasingly direct attention to the role that the wise play in the unfolding crisis. In the meantime, however, Daniel's perplexity about what he has seen invites further reflection on the meaning of his visions.

The paired visions in Daniel 7 and 8 stand out from the rest of the book. Both involve strange beasts and horns, symbols that we do not see anywhere else in Daniel. Although the creatures in chapter 7 are bizarre composites with features drawn from a variety of animals, while the beasts in chapter 8 are more recognizable as a ram and a goat, the two visions clearly have much in common. Both deal with similar historical periods, and both focus their attention on the final beast. The parallel between the two visions extends even further, however, for both also emphasize similar aspects of the beasts' destructiveness as they devour, crush, and destroy. Running roughshod over the earth, they trample other living creatures, and no one can rescue their victims from their power. Both visions dwell on the final beast's arrogant behavior against "the Most High" or "the Prince of princes," but even here they emphasize the beasts' power and violence, not merely their acts of sacrilege.

Like Daniel, the Jews in Antiochus' time lived in a world full of "bestial" confrontation. From the era of the Assyrian empire to their own day, their land had been repeatedly ravaged by warring powers.

Like Daniel, the Jews in Antiochus' time lived in a world full of "bestial" confrontation. From the era of the Assyrian empire in the eighth century to their own day, their land had been repeatedly overrun by warring powers, and their people had suffered the consequences of imperial brutality. Under Antiochus the violence became even greater. When Antiochus' armies set out from Syria to attack the Ptolemies in Egypt, they marched through the historic territory of Israel, raiding as they went. When Antiochus needed funds to pay for wars, he demanded more tribute money from the Jews and robbed the temple treasury in Jerusalem. Antiochus' actions followed and intensified a familiar pattern: imperial violence and greed devastated not just the fortresses and soldiers of the enemy nations, but the ordinary people living in the territories through which the armies passed. Innocent bystanders in the competing empires paid the price of their wars, and for the majority of the ordinary people living in Jerusalem and the surrounding area, life became little more than a daily struggle to feed themselves and their families.

The beasts in Daniel's visions are an apt symbol for the brutal behavior of economic and military superpowers in the present as well as in the distant past.

The beasts in Daniel's visions are an apt symbol for the brutal behavior of economic and military superpowers in the present as well as in the distant past. The military and economic violence of world powers continues to crush and destroy lives in our own time. Almost anywhere we look on the world stage, we see the price of war: missiles kill women, children, and the elderly; military blockades starve the innocent citizens of enemy countries; refugees fleeing invading armies live huddled in desolate tent camps; and nations spend far more tax money on weapons than on programs to feed the hungry and help the poor.

Although war rages in many parts of our world, it is far from the only evil that devastates peoples' lives today. We recently led a series of workshops for a group of leaders in an impoverished community in the Dominican Republic. The participants spoke frankly about the everyday challenges that they faced: no electricity, no clean water, little food, and too few jobs. They felt trapped, caught up in a corrupt and brutal system over which they had no power. Their lives were a microcosm of the experiences of the poor throughout the Dominican Republic. In the same way, the poor in the United States frequently express their sense that they are powerless before forces over which they have no control. Theologian William Stringfellow, who spent years working as a lawyer for street people, often heard them using animal imagery to describe their situation, speaking "of the gas company, the slum real estate lords, the social bureaucracies, the city administration, the Mafia, and police agencies as though they were predatory beasts, arrayed against the neighborhood and human beings, eating them alive."[10]

The beast symbolism in Daniel evokes the experiences of people throughout history whose lives are devoured, destroyed by economic, political, or military forces. The middle class as well as the poor may feel helpless before a brutal system. As the vision in Daniel 8 repeatedly emphasizes, the beasts charged in all directions and no one could rescue from their might. Nevertheless, at the same time that Daniel's visions highlight the ferocity of the beasts and the devastating consequences of the wars between them, they also stress that the beasts are neither ultimate nor eternal. They overrun and trample the earth, but only for a time. The predator soon becomes prey, as one beast succeeds another, and all fall under God's judgment. Only "the one like a human being" receives everlasting dominion.

The book of Daniel sets finite power struggles within the context of eternity. Through the symbolic language of apocalyptic visions, it exposes the life-denying hunger for power that characterized the successive empires of the ancient world and that still drives the imperial forces of our own time. Using the evocative images of the strange beasts with their threatening horns, it analyzes the factors motivating the resistance against Antiochus' pretensions and against the abusive and oppressive regime that he established. He came to the throne by usurping the place of the rightful heirs, and he maintained his power by usurping the religious rights of the people he ruled and by distorting and crushing their faith. The desecration of the temple sprang from a desire to destroy the entire culture and value system of a subject people—their whole traditional way of life. In the midst of this overwhelming situation, the book of Daniel speaks truth to power, revealing its limits and its self-destructive character, and reminding it that God's ends are utterly different from the ends of the empire.

The exhausting night of oppression under Antiochus IV Epiphanes had caused every glimmer of hope to disappear, but in the darkness there descends from the heavens a figure who brings hope. The visions in Daniel 7 and 8 teach us that both human beings and God have a role to play in human history. From our point of view in the midst of the struggle, it may seem as if we are utterly without power, helpless before political and economic forces over which we have no control. But as we watch the beasts fighting in the chaos and the dark, God's will for the world is revealed. In Daniel's night vision we see the mystery hidden behind the clouds—the majestic figure of "one like a human being," the prototype of God's goal for all humanity. Daniel's visions remind us that human beings are called to incarnate God's will. They invite us to dedicate ourselves to God's dream for the world, so that freed from the dehumanizing domination of evil, we may be restored to the liberty of God's children and empowered to exercise responsible stewardship over God's creation. Daniel's visions hold out hope for a disheartened people: as surely as the sun rises, at the end of the dark night will dawn God's new day.

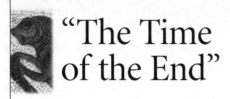 # "The Time of the End"

The bizarre visions of beasts leave Daniel greatly troubled. Confused and dismayed by the changing reality of a dark time, he does not know how to respond. In the first six chapters of Daniel, he and his friends have repeatedly been in danger but have always escaped, miraculously unharmed. Now the situation changes, as these final visions describe a time when even the educated elite will face persecution and death, although Daniel himself will remain alive. Scribes will become targets of imperial brutality and malice—"the wise among the people . . . shall fall by sword and flame, and suffer captivity and plunder" (11:33). How can Daniel go about the king's business in such a time? Where is the way forward?

In chapter 9 Daniel seeks God's presence in prayer. With God's help, in the deepest darkness he begins to see. The archangel Gabriel comes in response to his prayer, giving him understanding and showing him what lies ahead. Then, in a second vision, Daniel sees a mysterious heavenly figure: "I looked up and saw a man clothed in linen, with a belt of gold from Uphaz around his waist. His body was like beryl, his face like lightning, his eyes like flaming torches, his arms and legs like the gleam of burnished bronze, and the sound of his words like the roar of a multitude" (10:5–6). Daniel falls prostrate in terror, but the majestic visitor reassures him and delivers him from his paralyzing fear. With much more detail than in the previous visions, he gives Daniel a sweeping overview of scenes on the international stage from the time of Alexander the Great through his Ptolemaic and Seleucid successors, down to the time of Antiochus IV Epiphanes. Although the overview is presented as a prediction of what is to come, all but the last few verses (11:40–45) describe events that had already taken place by the time that the book of Daniel was written.

These final visions reflect the reality that scribes did not merely do the work that the king or their noble employers demanded of them as courtiers; they also had their own agendas. Some of them used their education and their influential positions for their own financial and political gain. Political maneuvering, bribery, and cutthroat competition among Jerusalem's educated elite played a significant role in provoking Antiochus' attacks on the city and on the temple. Many among the nobility, the priestly families, and the scribes who advised them cared for nothing but their own status and wealth and gave little thought to their religious obligations or to the common people whose livelihoods depended on the choices they made.

In the face of such evil, the final chapters of Daniel call those who remain loyal to God to "stand firm and take action" (11:32). Those who have the capacity to see the inner workings of power have a responsibility to speak the truth even if it costs them their lives. Although the scribes serve in the courts of nobles and kings, ultimately they will be punished or rewarded in a higher court. As Daniel's very name attests, "God is my judge." The rulers of earth may inflict torture and death on their subjects, but they will be held accountable by an eternal Sovereign. Death is not the end of the story.

Daniel's Repentance

This last section of the book, with its intense focus on history and politics, begins with Daniel's confession of sin before God.

These final chapters of the book, with their intense focus on history and politics, begin with Daniel's confession of sin before God. During the first year that Darius is on the throne, the story unfolds,

> I, Daniel, perceived in the books the number of years that, according to the word of the Lord to the prophet Jeremiah, must be fulfilled for the devastation of Jerusalem, namely, seventy years. (9:2)

Daniel is referring to Jeremiah's prophecy during the exile that after Jerusalem has lain devastated for seventy years after the Babylonian destruction, God would finally punish the Babylonians (Jeremiah 25:11–12; 29:10). Here Darius is described as the one "who became king over the realm of the Chaldeans," or Babylonians, thus reminding us that—at least according to the book of Daniel's version of history—it was Darius who overthrew the powers that conquered Judah and devastated Jerusalem. Daniel is not celebrating the fall of Babylon, however; in this first year of Darius' reign, the regime has changed but Jerusalem still lies in ruins and the people of Judah are still in exile, subject to the tyrannical whims of a foreign king. Not incidentally, Darius was also the king who threw Daniel to the lions because he persisted in praying to God in defiance of a royal edict.

Now Daniel once again turns to God in prayer, fasting in sackcloth and ashes. Yet he is not, as the NRSV has it, seeking "an answer" (9:3), for that is not in the Hebrew text. Rather the Hebrew says that Daniel turns his face toward God to *seek*, obeying the spirit of Jeremiah's prophecy: "If you seek me with all your heart, I will let you find me, says the LORD, and I will restore your fortunes" (Jeremiah 29:13–14). In prayer and supplication, Daniel is seeking not answers, but God's own presence.

The language of Daniel's prayer is both more elegant and more archaic than the rest of the Hebrew in the book: "'Ah, Lord, great and awesome God, keeping covenant and steadfast love with those who love you and keep your commandments, we have sinned and done wrong, acted wickedly and rebelled'" (9:4–5). It uses phrases and expressions that would have been familiar to the book's first readers from worship in the temple, in both structure and content strongly resembling other biblical texts such as the prayer of Ezra at a time of national lamentation in Nehemiah 9. In effect, Daniel prays in what we might call "King James" Hebrew, the heart language of the Jewish people.

We have seen that the literary setting is the first year of Darius' reign, but the whole prayer works equally well in the later context of life under Antiochus IV Epiphanes. By Antiochus' time, whole centuries, not just seventy years, have come and gone since Jeremiah made his prophecy, and God's people are still subject to a foreign king. Once again, Jerusalem has been devastated and the sanctuary lies desolate, unusable for worship. Furthermore, clues in Daniel 9:7 hint at the speaker's true location: "Open shame . . . falls on us, the people of Judah, the inhabitants of Jerusalem, and all Israel, those who are near and those who are far away, in all the lands to which you have driven *them*" (emphasis ours). Daniel speaks in the *first* person when mentioning the people of Judah and the inhabitants of Jerusalem, but in the *third* when referring to the exiles, so the author of the prayer lives in Jerusalem, not Babylon. Furthermore, he prays not that the exiles will be allowed to return to Jerusalem—as we might expect if he were in fact writing from Babylon—but that God's face will shine on the profaned sanctuary and that God will look upon the desolation and at the city that bears God's name.

Although Daniel is alone, he prays on behalf of his whole nation, confessing their sin as well as his own: "We have sinned and done wrong. . . . We have not listened to your servants the prophets. . . . Open shame, O LORD, falls on us, our kings, our officials, and our ancestors, because we have sinned against you" (9:5–8). By praying in the first person plural, Daniel takes responsibility for being complicit in the sins that affect a whole society. The bestial imagery in chapters 7 and 8 highlighted the fact that people often feel helpless before systems and powers that show no concern for human life, but it is equally true that these oppressive powers would be toothless if no one participated or obeyed. Daniel owns up to the reality that through his own actions and his silent acceptance of the destructive and life-denying actions of others, he participates in corporate sin.

In his confession Daniel repeatedly mentions the covenant and the law, drawing a direct line between his people's failure to keep God's commandments and the disaster that has befallen Jerusalem. At the end of the covenant renewal ceremony in Deuteronomy, Moses told the people that they would be cursed with disaster, conquest, exile, and occupation by foreign powers if they failed to obey God's law. Shortly before the Babylonian conquest, the prophet Jeremiah also pronounced the covenant curse on the people of Judah, proclaiming on God's behalf that because they had refused to heed God's voice, "I brought upon them all the words of this covenant, which I commanded them to do, but they did not" (Jeremiah 11:8). Now, recalling the words of these earlier prophets, Daniel acknowledges that the choices he and his people made have provoked the current crisis. All

Recalling the words of these earlier prophets, Daniel acknowledges that the choices he and his people made have provoked the current crisis.

the curses of the law of Moses have been visited on Daniel and his contemporaries because of their disobedience. Moreover, Daniel's repeated reference to Israel's kings and leaders in his penitential prayer suggests that, since they are the ones to whom the prophets spoke most directly, they bear special responsibility for Israel's failure to keep the covenant even though all Israel shares the blame

Although Daniel's words are clearly a confession of sin, they are also a confession of faith in the God who judges in order to save. The whole prayer stresses God's greatness, mercy, and steadfast love. Daniel approaches God with utter confidence that God will hear and answer. He makes no excuses for sinning, no attempt to persuade God that he and the people deserve to be forgiven. On the contrary, he admits that they deserve punishment. Nevertheless, he asks for mercy both for himself and for his people, in the confidence that God's righteous acts are intimately linked not simply with judgment, but with forgiveness. Daniel bases his plea on nothing more or less than God's own character: "We do not present our supplication before you on the ground of our righteousness, but on the ground of your great mercies" (9:18). His words find an echo in "The Prayer of Humble Access" that appears in the eucharistic liturgy in many editions of the Book of Common Prayer: "We do not presume to come to this thy Table, O merciful Lord, trusting in our own righteousness, but in thy manifold and great mercies. We are not worthy so much as to gather up the crumbs under thy Table. But thou art the same Lord whose property is always to have mercy." God forgives not because human beings deserve it, therefore, but because compassion is an essential aspect of the divine nature. God's righteousness is revealed in mercy.

By approaching the "great and awesome God" in prayer and worship, confessing Israel's sin and God's righteousness, Daniel shows appropriate humility before the divine presence. Despite the extraordinary faithfulness that he has demonstrated in the first half of Daniel, he makes no claim that he deserves any special treatment from God. Consequently Daniel's words and actions stand in stark contrast to the little horn with the mouth that speaks "arrogantly" in chapter 7 and the king of bold countenance who is great in his own mind in chapter 8. On the other hand, though Daniel is humble and contrite, freely admitting his failure and sin, he does not grovel or demean himself or his people as worthless. Instead, he approaches God boldly, confident that God will act to save the city and the people that bear the divine name.

While he is still praying, Gabriel appears and begins to speak with him. Several details about his arrival are noteworthy. First, Daniel describes him as "the man Gabriel, whom I had seen before in a vision" (9:21), thus emphasizing the messenger's human appearance and reminding us of his interpretation of Daniel's vision of the ram and the goat. Second, Gabriel comes at the time of the evening sacrifice, or—since the temple lies desolate and no sacrifices are being offered—at the time when the evening sacrifice would normally take place. Clearly, God hears and answers prayer even when the faithful cannot offer sacrifice. Finally, Daniel repeatedly emphasizes that Gabriel appears during his prayer, while he is still speaking and not after he has finished praying. In other words, Daniel has only to ask and God responds at once.

Gabriel's first words emphasize the depiction of God as compassionate and attentive to Daniel's prayer, for the angel has come to give him wisdom and understanding. In fact, the message he bears was sent at the moment that Daniel began to pray—"You are greatly beloved" (9:23). The divine response does not come because of pleading or persuasion; God answers immediately because God treasures Daniel.

The rest of Gabriel's message focuses on the question Daniel identified at the beginning of the chapter: Jeremiah's prophecy that after seventy years, God would punish the Babylonians, bring the exiles home, and restore the fortunes of Judah. By one measure Jeremiah's prophecy was accurate: the first temple was destroyed in 587/6 BCE, and the second temple was dedicated in 516 BCE. The problem was that the prophecy remained only partially and very unsatisfactorily fulfilled. In all likelihood Jeremiah's original prediction of a seventy-year exile was symbolic, representing an average human lifespan rather than an exact length of time. But many generations later, in the mid-second century when Daniel was written, God's people were still waiting for the fulfillment of the rest of the prophecy. Jerusalem remained subject to foreign domination and Judah's fortunes were far from restored. How much longer would they have to wait for the peace and prosperity that Jeremiah had prophesied?

In response, Gabriel addresses the theological issues raised by the ongoing experience of exile: how long will the exile last, and why must God's people endure this period of suffering? Gabriel answers the first question by reinterpreting the seventy years as "seventy weeks of years," that is, seventy times seven, or 490. The seventy weeks recall both the Jubilee year, which is to be celebrated every seven weeks of years, and the warning that if the people disobey God's commandments and fail to keep the Jubilee, God will punish them sevenfold for their sins (Leviticus 26:17–45). Then Gabriel explains the purpose of the seventy weeks of years, which is "to finish the transgression, to put an end to sin, and to atone for iniquity, to bring in everlasting righteousness, to seal both vision and prophet, and to anoint a most holy place" (9:24). The long wait for deliverance is a time both of endings and of new beginnings.

The phrase "the transgression," which occurs only here and in 8:13, clearly refers to Antiochus IV Epiphanes' desecration of the temple in Jerusalem. By Antiochus' command, over the altar of burnt offering in God's sanctuary stands an abomination that "desolates" (from the Hebrew verb *shamem*), on which people offer sacrifice to Zeus Olympius, known locally as Baal Shamem. At this moment the sanctuary is desolate, but God has decreed the end of the "desolator" (*shomem*).

The seventy weeks of years are a time to "finish the transgression," "put an end to sin," and "atone for iniquity." Daniel's confession suggests that the many years in exile have taught the scribes to recognize their sinfulness and their unfaithfulness. When God first delivered the people of Israel from Egypt, they could not accept the

> *The seventy weeks of years are a time to "finish the transgression," "put an end to sin," and "atone for iniquity."*

divine gift of freedom. They considered God's provision of food, water, and guidance through the wilderness inadequate, so they rebelled and made their own gods; only long after did they learn to depend on God to meet their needs. Similarly, during the exile, when God's people were subjugated by a series of cruel and powerful kings, they forgot God and began worshipping the gods of their oppressors—gods like Baal Shamem. But now it is time to be done with transgression and idolatry. Now, at long last, the extended journey through the wilderness of exile has enabled some of the inhabitants of Jerusalem and Judah to arrive at a deeper understanding both of God and of their own role as God's people. Through their patient endurance of suffering, the scribes who wrote Daniel's confession have learned to know the compassion, love, and justice of God. They realize that until God's people trust that love and justice, they will not be ready to live into God's promise of freedom.

The seventy weeks of years is a time not only for endings, but for new revelations of God's power to heal and restore. God intends to "bring in everlasting righteousness." The period of exile will culminate in events that "seal both vision and prophet," confirming the authenticity both of Jeremiah's prophecy and of Daniel's vision in the previous chapter. The sanctuary lies desolate now, but God will remove its uncleanness and anoint a holy of holies. Although Daniel still lives in exile, the promised end is drawing near.

Gabriel concludes his message by overviewing the cataclysmic events that are to take place during the seventy weeks of years. Although much ink has been spilled by scholars trying to determine the exact beginning and ending dates of this 490-year period, no consensus has been reached. Like Jeremiah's original reference to seventy years, the number is probably more symbolic than literal. Many scholars identify the anointed prince (*mashiach nagid*, which can also be translated "anointed leader" or "anointed ruler") whom Gabriel refers to in 9:26 as Cyrus the Great, while others identify him as Joshua, the high priest described in Zechariah 3. The "sixty-two weeks of years" during which Jerusalem is rebuilt refers to the long period after the return from exile and the rededication of the temple, when Jerusalem had been rebuilt but still was controlled by foreign rulers.

Gabriel pays little attention to the first sixty-nine weeks, however, focusing instead on the final week—a seven-year period of destruction, war, and "an abomination that desolates." His description is one of the passages most widely used by interpreters who insist that the book of Daniel is about the end of the world and the second coming of Jesus. Hal Lindsey and many others understand the claim that "its end shall come with a flood, and to the end there shall be war" as describing the same traumatic period of earthquakes, wars, and famines that Jesus mentions in Mark's gospel. Since Jesus is clearly alluding to Daniel when he mentions "the desolating sacrilege set up where it ought not to be" (Mark 13:14), it is natural to perceive some connection between the passages. As we have seen, in Daniel "the desolating sacrilege" or "abomination that desolates" refers to the altar of Zeus that Antiochus built over the altar of burnt offering in the temple. In Mark, it alludes to a second desecration of the holy place, either by Zealots who turned the temple into an arms depot and fortress during their revolt against Rome in 65–70 CE, or by Romans who entered, defiled, and eventually destroyed the temple. By contrast, Lindsey and readers like him ignore the historical references and understand both Daniel 9 and Mark 13 to be predicting the birth pangs that will precede the end of the world. Here, however, Gabriel is talking not about the end of time, but about the end of Antiochus IV Epiphanes and about several incidents that took place during his reign.

> "The desolating sacrilege" or "abomination that desolates" refers to the altar of Zeus that Antiochus built over the altar of burnt offering in the temple.

A little historical and cultural background will help to clarify his message and explain why Gabriel chooses to use a dating system that recalls the biblical law of Jubilee. When the Ptolemies controlled Jerusalem and the historic land of Israel during the third century, they set up a system of tax farming whereby noble Jewish families managed large tracts of land and collected taxes on the produce. Any money that they collected above and beyond the prescribed amount destined for the Pharaoh in Egypt went into their own pockets. During this period the high priest in Jerusalem served both as the religious leader and as the designated local political authority over the Jewish population in Jerusalem and the surrounding area. In his capacity as high priest, he managed the tithes and offerings on which the temple and its priests depended. Furthermore, the Ptolemaic kings counted on him to maintain order and to make sure that tribute payments and farm taxes arrived in a timely fashion. As a result, the high priest enjoyed considerable status, power, and wealth, not least because he managed and profited from the tax farming system. Although tax farming enriched the aristocracy, it crushed the peasants, many of whom had to take out loans to pay their debts, while some were forced into debt slavery.

Then the balance of power in Jerusalem began to shift. Joseph—a member of a family known as the Tobiads that traced its lineage to Jordan and that had intermarried with the high priestly family generations earlier—worked his way into the inner circles of the Ptolemaic court. Joseph and his sons were Hellenized aristocrats who knew how to work the levers of power and were perfectly willing to compromise their religious principles for a profit. Through expensive gifts and promises to double the tax revenue, Joseph persuaded the king to entrust him, and not his uncle the high priest, with the responsibility for collecting taxes throughout the region. As a result, he and his family became enormously wealthy and powerful, and the noble families in Jerusalem had to navigate through treacherous waters in order to maintain the favor of both the Tobiad tax collectors and the Oniad high priests. Furthermore, the peasants who farmed the land were now caught between competing systems of taxation that bled them dry.

Toward the turn of the second century BCE, it became evident that the Seleucids' star was rising. Some members of the Jerusalem aristocracy remained loyal to the Ptolemies, but many others began preparing for the coming regime change by shifting their allegiance. When a Seleucid army arrived in Jerusalem, the nobles who controlled the city welcomed the troops with open arms, provided them with lavish provisions, and joined them in attacking the Ptolemaic garrison that remained in the city. Subsequently, Antiochus III returned the local oversight of religious and secular matters to the high priest. The Jerusalem temple and the priestly families who ran it once again managed both the temple funds and the imperial tax revenue. The temple itself functioned not only as a place of worship, but as a bank, and wealthy families put their money in its treasury for safekeeping.

Seleucus IV, the successor of Antiochus III, continued his father's policy toward Jerusalem and its high priest. By this time, however, the tensions among Jerusalem's noble families had risen from a simmer to a boil. A temple official named Simon became angry with Onias III, the high priest, over the administration of the city market. Seeking revenge against Onias, he told the Seleucid authorities that the temple treasury contained untold wealth. According to a legend in 2 Maccabees 3, the emissary whom Seleucus IV sent to collect funds from the treasury was miraculously prevented from entering the treasury, and thus the sanctity of the temple was preserved, at least for a time. Nevertheless, the infighting among the Jewish aristocracy first brought the Jerusalem temple treasury to the Seleucids' attention.

The Jerusalem temple and the priestly families who ran it managed both the temple funds and the imperial tax revenue. The temple functioned not only as a place of worship, but as a bank, where wealthy families put their money in the temple treasury for safekeeping.

When Antiochus IV came to the Seleucid throne in 175 BCE, he was in serious financial trouble; his predecessors had lost several important battles to the Romans and as a result the kingdom owed the Romans heavy tribute. Recognizing an opportunity, Onias' own brother Jason raised an enormous sum of money and bribed the new king to make him high priest instead, promising to raise a fortune in tribute money. He also assured Antiochus that he would turn Jerusalem into a Greek polis, build a gymnasium next to the temple, and enroll the cream of the Jerusalem population as citizens of Antioch. Under his leadership, a new secular constitution derived from the traditions of the Greek city-states replaced the ancestral laws of the Jews. As a result of Jason's treachery, Onias III was forced to flee for his life.

Three years later, Menelaus, the brother of the temple official Simon, outbid Jason for the high priesthood. While he was in Antioch, delivering the tribute money that Jason had sent to Antiochus IV, he pledged to increase the tribute from the Jews by three hundred talents if the king would make him high priest. Although Menelaus was not even of high priestly lineage, Antiochus gave him the job, but the new high priest soon found that he could not easily carry out

his promise. Instead, he resorted to stealing temple funds and brib-
ing imperial officials. When word of this came to Onias III in exile,
he reported the bribes to the Seleucid authorities and was afterwards
assassinated. That is the meaning of Gabriel's prophecy, for Onias
III—the anointed high priest and leader of the people—is "an
anointed one who shall be cut off and shall have nothing" (9:26).

In 170 BCE Antiochus IV tried to improve his financial situation
and increase his power by attacking Egypt. His first campaign was
successful, and he returned loaded down with treasure, passing
through Jerusalem on his way back from Egypt and stealing the valuables from the temple. Two years later, he launched a second campaign against Egypt, but this time, after some initial successful
battles, he was stopped in his tracks by the Romans. A Roman envoy
bearing orders from the Senate commanded him to take his troops
and go home.

Meanwhile, Jason, thinking that Antiochus was dead, seized the
opportunity and returned to Jerusalem with an army of supporters.
Menelaus and his followers retreated to the citadel. When Antiochus
heard, he recognized a chance to recoup some of his financial losses
and recover his pride. He sent a large army to attack Jerusalem, which
was heavily damaged in the battle. His forces looted the temple, stole
all its valuables and the contents of the temple treasury, and halted
the daily offerings to Yahweh. To crown the offense, they set the altar
of Zeus Olympius/Baal Shamem over the altar of burnt offering, and
then sacrificed a pig on it. Then they tore down the fortifications
around the temple and built a new fortress—the Akra—on a location that overlooked the temple mount.

These are the events described in the final verses of Daniel 9: "The
troops of the prince who is to come shall destroy the city and the
sanctuary." For the population of Jerusalem, Gabriel's prediction of
endless warfare must have rung very true. Caught between the
Ptolemies and the Seleucids, trapped even between competing high
priests, they had suffered one military incursion after another. For
those who lived through this time, deciphering Gabriel's words
would have been easy: Antiochus IV was the prince who destroyed
their city. He made a covenant with the many in Jerusalem who supported Hellenistic reform, and for three and a half years ("half of the

week") banned sacrifices and offerings, putting in place "the abomination that desolates." But for Jews still suffering under his brutal reign, Gabriel's message brought hope: "the decreed end" will be "poured out upon the desolator."

Gabriel's words are more than a judgment on Antiochus IV, however. By describing the exile as seventy weeks of years, he recalls the biblical law of Jubilee and condemns the leaders of Israel for failing to put it in practice. According to Leviticus 25, after seven weeks of years—forty-nine years—all land must be returned to its original owners, those who have sold themselves into debt slavery must be set free, and loans must be forgiven. The land must lie fallow for a full year, and those who work it are to rest. At stake in the law are basic biblical principles: the land belongs to God, and its people belong to God. "For they are my servants, whom I brought out of the land of Egypt; they shall not be sold as slaves are sold. You shall not rule over them with harshness, but shall fear your God" (Leviticus 25:42–43).

> By describing the exile as seventy weeks of years, Gabriel recalls the biblical law of Jubilee and condemns the leaders of Israel for failing to put it in practice.

The system of tax farming that brought wealth and power to the aristocrats in Jerusalem violated both the spirit and the letter of Jubilee. Jerusalem's noble families have cared for no one but themselves and their own profit, enriching themselves at the expense of the common people of the land—God's own people. Moreover, the high priests and the priestly families who should be responsible for ensuring that the law of Jubilee is practiced are not merely implicated in violating the law; they are among its chief violators. But judgment is coming, and soon God will "proclaim liberty throughout the land to all its inhabitants" (Leviticus 25:10).

"A Man Clothed in Linen"

> In the third year of King Cyrus of Persia a word was revealed to Daniel, who was named Belteshazzar. The word was true, and it concerned a great conflict. He understood the word, having received understanding in the vision. (10:1)

Now the visionary scene changes to the third year of King Cyrus' reign. The details given at the beginning of the scene emphasize the theme of ongoing exile that have already been raised. After Daniel "who was named Belteshazzar" has been fasting for three weeks, on the twenty-fourth day of the first month (24 Nisan in the Jewish calendar), a mysterious visitor appears to him while he is standing beside the Tigris River. Although Cyrus is the king famously associated with sending the Jews back to Jerusalem and ending the exile, Daniel is still known by his captive name. Furthermore, he has fasted right through Passover, which is celebrated from 15–21 Nisan (Leviticus 23:5–6). How can he celebrate the Jews' liberation from slavery when they still serve a foreign king? His location "on the bank of the great river (that is, the Tigris)" suggests that the seat of foreign power has moved from Babylon, where Nebuchadnezzar had his capital beside the "great river" Euphrates, to Syria, where the Seleucids established their first capital beside the Tigris.

After Daniel's extended period of fasting, he sees an awe-inspiring vision of "a man clothed in linen, with a belt of gold from Uphaz around his waist" (10:5). The description of the man's physical appearance ("his body was like beryl, his face like lightning, his eyes like flaming torches") recalls Ezekiel's initial vision of the throne chariot and the living creatures, but his clothes are equally significant; he is dressed like a priest who serves at the altar. In the prophecy of Ezekiel, God commands a "man clothed in linen, with a writing case at his side" (9:3) to go through Jerusalem and put a mark on the forehead of everyone who mourned for the evil that had been done within it. All those who did not bear the mark were to be killed. Similarly, the man whom Daniel sees is associated with books and writing, for he has been sent to tell the sage "what is inscribed in the book of truth" (10:21).

The previous messenger in Daniel was identified as Gabriel, but this mysterious figure remains unnamed. When he appears, Daniel turns pale with terror, and when he begins to speak, Daniel falls into a trance, completely overcome. Then an unidentified hand touches him to reassure him, and the man speaks again, telling Daniel that he is greatly beloved and that from the first day that he sought to learn and to humble himself before God, his words have been heard. His words depict Daniel as the prototype of the faithful scribe, humble and dedicated to studying until he understands. Like Gabriel, the man dressed in linen has been sent in response to Daniel's words, to help Daniel understand what will happen to his people.

Like Gabriel, the man dressed in linen has been sent in response to Daniel's words, to help Daniel understand what will happen to his people.

Several details about Daniel's interactions with his heavenly visitor deserve comment. First, Daniel's account of the vision emphasizes the figure's human appearance and his gentle concern for Daniel. He is described various times as "a man," and he comforts Daniel, telling him not to be afraid and assuring him repeatedly that he is greatly loved. Twice this "one in human form" touches Daniel, first touching his lips so that he is able to speak, a gesture that reminds us of the calling of the prophet Isaiah, and then strengthening him. It is not clear whether this being in human form is the same person who first speaks to Daniel or someone else, but whether Daniel sees one person or two, the emphasis on his human appearance recalls the "one like a human being" in chapter 7. Although Daniel is overcome by fear, his encounter with the divine messenger strengthens him and gives him courage.

This figure tells Daniel that his arrival was delayed because the prince of the kingdom of Persia opposed him, and he was able to come only after the archangel Michael arrived to carry on the battle. Later the fight will resume, first with the prince of Persia and then with the prince of Greece—"There is no one with me who contends against these princes except Michael, your prince" (10:21). In this way the rulers who oppress Israel have cosmic counterparts against which God's armies do battle, and the mysterious figure who speaks to Daniel moves in a realm of heavenly powers that are the counterparts of those on earth. Daniel's vision reminds us that God does not abandon humans to fight evil alone. Although we may feel helpless, dominated by faceless systems of oppression over which we have no control, God is at work to destroy the evil systems themselves, not merely the humans who may hold a powerful position in them for a time.

At this point Daniel's visitor provides him with an overview of international history from the Persian period through the time of Antiochus IV, ending with a prediction of Antiochus' own death. After mentioning three more kings who will arise in Persia, he describes a warrior king whose kingdom is divided and distributed among others who are not of his blood—clearly meaning Alexander the Great and the generals who fought over his empire after his death. Then follows a remarkably detailed and accurate history lesson, which summarizes the reign of the Ptolemies (the kings of the south) and the Seleucids (the kings of the north) from the time of Ptolemy I until the death of Antiochus III, with "the beautiful land" of Israel caught between the warring parties (11:5–19). The messenger concludes the story leading up to the reign of Antiochus IV with his predecessor, Seleucus IV, who tried to rob the temple treasury and soon after was assassinated (11:20).

This is history told for a purpose—in his penetrating critique of the greed and lust for power behind international politics, the "man clothed in linen" exposes the manipulation and deceit that run rampant among the nobles and the economic elites not only in Egypt and Syria, but in Jerusalem as well. The remainder of the divine messenger's historical overview focuses on Antiochus IV Epiphanes, his wars with Egypt and his attacks on Jerusalem. But what is most important in this passage are not the details about his campaigns, but the emphasis on Antiochus' treachery, the complicity of Jerusalem's nobility, and the role of the wise. From the beginning, Daniel's visitor focuses on Antiochus' political machinations—he comes to the throne not by legitimate succession, but "through intrigue," forms alliances, "acts deceitfully," gains the support of the richest men of the province by "lavishing plunder, spoil, and wealth on them," and sits at table with his enemy to "exchange lies" (11:21–27). In other words, Antiochus does not simply overpower the nobles and rulers on whom his continued success depends, but also uses wealth and deception to buy their cooperation.

When the "man clothed in linen" turns his attention to Antiochus' most recent history, he pulls no punches: Jerusalem's own leaders are implicated in the desolation of their religious tradition and their holy city. The divine visitor describes Antiochus' humiliating encounter with the Romans and his subsequent attack on Jerusalem and the temple. Paying heed to "those who forsake the holy covenant" (11:30)—the Hellenizing faction among the Jerusalem nobility—Antiochus begins a brutal crackdown against those who remain faithful to the Torah.

Like the priests who forsake the covenant in order to enrich and empower themselves, Antiochus does not respect the gods of his ancestors. In his own eyes, he is "greater than any god" (11:36), and religion is merely a tool; instead of worshipping the traditional gods of the Seleucids—Apollo and Adonis/Tammuz—he honors "the god of fortresses" (11:38). In a polytheistic era, each culture and city had its own favorite gods, and competing loyalties could cause problems. But the mercenary troops whom Antiochus installed in the citadel overlooking the Jerusalem temple could all agree on at least one god: they worshipped Baal Shamem, the warrior god, the god of fortresses. Antiochus' decision to build an altar to Zeus Olympius/Baal Shamem over the altar of burnt offering is strategic, because it helps him unify his troops.

Despite his desecration of all that the faithful people of Israel hold sacred, he is able to exploit many members of Jerusalem's ruling families for his own ends, seducing "with intrigue those who violate the covenant" (11:32). How does he win and keep their support? "Those who acknowledge him he shall make more wealthy, and shall appoint them as rulers over many, and shall distribute the land for a price" (11:39). The reference to the Tobiad family and to Jason, Menelaus, and their supporters could hardly be more obvious. Is there anything that they would be unwilling to do in exchange for control over the tax farm system or appointment as high priest? Profit and power are at stake, and little else matters to them.

As these historical overviews show, the crisis under Antiochus had its origins in events that took place long before his birth. Antiochus inherited his predecessor's war debt and had to contend with a political and economic situation that had developed over centuries. He did not begin the wars between the Ptolemids and Seleucids, or establish the policy of tax farming, or start the rivalries between the Tobiads and the Oniads, but merely adapted to and took advantage of the existing realities. Although he was the most conspicuous actor, in the end he was only one powerful player in an entire system, who would not have been able to accomplish all that he did without the collusion of the competing factions within the Jerusalem aristocracy. Furthermore, this system of power dynamics preexisted him and would continue after his death. But the game stops if enough players refuse to play.

The book of Daniel challenges the faithful scribes to stop playing the game. As Daniel's heavenly visitor says, "The people who are loyal to their God shall stand firm and take action. The wise among the people shall give understanding to many" (11:32–33). Nothing in Daniel suggests that this is a call to armed resistance. Nor is this mere passivity, waiting on God to act while they continue with their lives as if nothing has happened. On the contrary, the wisest and most faithful scribes are being called not just to contemplate and confess the sovereignty of God, but to put their beliefs into practice. They are being challenged to put their service to God above their loyalty to their employers. The educated elite are to use their skills and their training to give understanding to others. They work within the courts and see the political maneuvering that takes place behind the scenes. Because they advise the high priests and the tax farmers, the Hellenists and their opponents, keeping the books and recording the financial transactions, they more than anyone else have the perspective and the education to understand the system and to expose how it works. If they shine the light of day into the dark corners where secret deals are made, the dealmakers' greed and dishonesty become visible to everyone. Words are a powerful weapon.

But revealing private treachery to the public eye is risky business. The scribes' weapons may be nonviolent, but the response of the powerful is not. When the wise stand firm in their resolve, they pay the price for their courage—"they shall fall by sword and flame, and suffer captivity and plunder." The phrase "they shall receive a little help" (11:34) has often been taken as suggesting that the scribes were ambivalent toward the Maccabean revolt, but more recent research suggests that the book of Daniel may well have been completed before the revolt began, and that the phrase should be translated "they shall receive little help," meaning that few others will assist them. This interpretation fits well with the next line, "and many shall join them insincerely." The scribes' resistance is costly and dangerous. Some of the wise lose their positions and their possessions; some are thrown into prison; and some die. Many who say they will support them in their stand against the powers that be flee at the first sign of danger. Persecution tests the faithful. It refines and purifies them, so that only what is most valuable in them remains.

Daniel's mysterious visitor speaks frankly about the conse-quences of standing up to Antiochus IV Epiphanes and his allies, but he also holds out hope. Toward the end of chapter 11, he leaves the historical narrative behind and predicts the future, outlining a series of events that will lead to Antiochus' death. Until this point, his description of Antiochus' life has been impressively accurate, but according to other historical records, the scenario that he lays out at the end of Daniel 11 is purely speculative. After his desecra-tion of the temple, Antiochus IV did not go to war with the Ptolemies again, and he died in Persia rather than in Palestine. The inaccuracy of this final prediction supports the conclusion that the book of Daniel was written before Antiochus died in 164 BCE, but the messenger is at least partially correct—Antiochus' reign of ter-ror is soon to end.

"Like the Stars Forever and Ever"

Now an angelic figure repeats the question that we first heard in chapter 8: "How long?" "How long shall it be until the end of these wonders?" (12:6). His words give voice to the heartfelt cry of God's persecuted people: how long must we wait, how long will the suffer-ing continue, how long until God acts to save us? The man clothed in linen raises his hands to heaven and swears that it will be "for a time, two times, and half a time," mysterious words that he later interprets both as 1,290 days and as 1,335 days. In other words, although the persecution of God's people and the desolation of Jerusalem is not yet over, it will last for only about three and a half more years. His prediction agrees with information from other his-torical sources, since the temple was desecrated in 167 BCE and rededicated in 164 BCE.

The divine messenger speaks a powerful word of hope for those who are still risking everything in their stand against evil: only a lit-tle longer and their suffering will end; only a little longer, and God will save them. But what of those who have already paid the price for their faithfulness? What of those who have died? How can God allow Menelaus, Jason, and their supporters to become wealthy and pow-erful, while scribes who resisted and denounced them have been tor-tured and killed? Where is God's justice?

For this question, too, the man in linen has a surprising answer: "Many of those who sleep in the dust of the earth shall awake, some to everlasting life, and some to shame and everlasting contempt. Those who are wise shall shine like the brightness of the sky, and those who lead many to righteousness, like the stars forever and ever" (12:2–3). This may be the first reference in the Bible to a final judgment, and perhaps resurrection and a life after death. Daniel's vision of a judgment after death is not fully developed, but remains tantalizingly indefinite. Yet it opens the door for the later belief in a general resurrection, and its overall message is clear:

> There shall be a time of anguish, such as has never occurred since nations first came into existence. But at that time your people shall be delivered, everyone who is found written in the book. (12:1)

Death is not the end. The wicked will be punished, even though they may seem to be thriving now. Those who remained faithful even to the point of death will be rewarded with everlasting life. The eternal judge, the Ancient One whose kingdom endures forever, will have the last word.

The scribes who wrote Daniel knew that although they served in human courts, ultimately they were accountable to the divine judge. The whole book is a message to the wise, challenging them to use their education and their gifts not simply to benefit themselves or their employers, but in the service of God. The scribal authors wrote so that others could profit from their insights into life in the courts of the nobles—the vices and fears of the kings, their weaknesses and doubts, and the arrogance that prevented them from exercising true leadership. Scribes preserved the traditions of the past, but they were also the teachers who trained future leaders. They had the resources to help future kings develop new and more just forms of government. Through their influence they could prevent abuses and shape policies that would help farmers and laborers, aliens, widows and children, and the poorest of the poor.

The court stories in the first half of Daniel and the visions in the last half call the educated to use their knowledge for the common good.

The court stories in the first half of Daniel and the visions in the last half call the educated to use their knowledge for the common good. As a character, Daniel models the disciplines that the educated must practice for the benefit of the larger society. As a scholar he studies the wisdom of the past—both his own traditions and those outside Israel—in order to bring together the most important insights from a variety of cultures. As a leader he shrewdly observes the reality of the present, learning the way that the world works, discerning the motives of those who hold political and religious authority, and examining the techniques others use to manipulate others and win their support. Daniel honors the lives and needs of the poor, reminding the powerful that those who live under their shadow are God's creatures, and that the earth's resources are gifts from God to be used for the good of all. He prays not simply in times of need, but as a regular discipline, separating himself from distractions in order to perceive himself and the world more clearly, and confessing his faith in the God who is at work to transform the kingdoms of this world into the reign of God. Daniel works within the realities of the existing society, seeking to bend them toward justice, but when he must, he breaks with the existing systems and boldly speaks truth to power. When it is necessary, he takes his stand alongside all the faithful witnesses, living and dead, who have offered up their lives in order to worship the true God, not the false images before which the earthly powers bow down.

The book of Daniel is a ringing reminder that the empires of this world come and go, but God's reign is eternal. Although its utopic vision of history's culmination is not fully achievable at present, the final revelation of salvation will arrive at the moment that God chooses. At that time God will be revealed as the ruler of history whose sovereignty endures forever. Meanwhile, God is the future in whom we wait. We live in hope, believing God's promise and knowing God's faithfulness.

Daniel calls us to stop worshipping our own images, to stop bowing down to wealth and our desire for power, and to worship God alone. It teaches us that corruption and political dishonesty and the abuse of the poor persist not simply because the powerful inflict them, but because the rest of us let them. Inaction is consent. Those who see must stand firm and take action, exposing the evil systems that destroy human lives.

From beginning to end, Daniel calls us to place our lives in God's care, trusting the one who gives us all that we need and who comforts and strengthens us when we are too weak and afraid to hear the divine word. It shows us God's dream for humanity and assures us that we are greatly beloved. It invites us to live into God's vision of another possible world, God's own reign of justice and peace. And when we have offered all that we have to God, it speaks a final word: "But you, go your way, and rest; you shall rise for your reward at the end of the days" (12:13).

ACKNOWLEDGMENTS

Writing a book is both a social undertaking and a lonely process. It is social because every book depends on the wisdom of many people besides its authors, and it is lonely because, when all is said and done, the authors have to hole up in a room by themselves and struggle with words until a book is born. We owe a great debt not only to those whose ideas are reflected in this book, but also to those who sacrificed so that we could have time and space to write it.

Our work on Daniel began as a series of Bible studies for the twice-yearly conferences of the Church in Metropolitan Areas Network. We would like to thank Bishop Mark Beckwith and the Rev. Geoffrey Curtiss for inviting us to lead the studies, and all our colleagues in the CMA network for offering your insights, challenging our interpretations, and sharing the unforgettable stories of your daily struggles and triumphs. We thank God for you and pray that you will continue to "be the heart of Jesus in the heart of the city."

The Rev. Christopher Johnson, the Social and Economic Justice Officer of the Episcopal Church, has been a blessing to both of us. His theological insights and reflections on biblical texts have stimulated our thinking, and because he has invited us to lead biblical and theological studies for several conferences, we have met new people from whom we have learned about a rich variety of ministries.

Our interpretation has been shaped by the work of many scholars besides those named in the footnotes and the suggestions for further reading. We have learned even from those with whose ideas we disagree—and perhaps especially from them.

We would like to thank Wartburg College for awarding Judith a faculty development grant. Wartburg's generosity made it possible for us to spend several weeks working together during a critical period in this coauthored project.

Our editor, Cynthia L. Shattuck, has guided us through the final stages of writing this book. She gently pointed out passages that needed revising, and we are deeply grateful for her ability to separate the straw from the gold. Her critical insights and excellent ear for language have been a great gift to us.

The last word of thanks goes to our friends and families. You have made the greatest sacrifices so that we could make this dream a reality. On too many occasions we have had to isolate ourselves and work on the book instead of spending time with you. Thank you for bearing with us through it all. Your love has sustained us, and now—at last—we are free to enjoy your company again.

STUDY QUESTIONS

Sharon Ely Pearson

The book of Daniel is full of stories, perhaps first learned in child-hood, as well as apocalyptic dreams and visions of the end times. It is a collection of tales from a time long ago, when stories were told to share deeper meaning of a reality that was too dangerous to openly talk about. These stories of danger and rescue, beasts and heavenly warriors can be read as myth, history, wisdom, or as many have stated throughout the years, as predictors of the destruction of the world. Can the stories of Daniel speak to us today?

Introduction

This study guide is meant to accompany each chapter as a means to go deeper and reflect upon the events, personalities and ideas that the author unpacks through the chapters of the book of Daniel. The questions and reflections will invite you into a conversation about how the practice of one's faith can continue while in exile, recogniz-ing the parallels between Daniel's situation and the challenges faced by Christians all around the world today. How we can practice our faith in a world that is increasingly secular, suspicious, and hostile to those who speak publicly about one's beliefs?

The entire book claims to take place in the sixth century BCE, culminating in "the third year of King Cyrus of Persia," 535 BCE. The structure of the book of Daniel is straightforward. It begins with six "court" tales from the Babylonian exile, written from a very Jew-ish point of view using a legendary hero who was taken captive in the exile as a young boy and brought up in the court of the Babylon-ian king. The second portion involves four visions in which Daniel learns about coming occurrences either in a dream or though an angel. These are also set during the Babylonian and early Persian years. The book ends with three additional stories showing Daniel's wisdom and faith with visions of the last times and final instructions. The book of Daniel is one of the later books of the Old Testament and has played an important part in later interpretation of the Bible, especially in Christian circles. It has many connections to the wisdom tradition, religious piety for the postexilic period, some of the earliest teachings about a divine promise of life after death, a coming kingdom of God, and apocalyptic prophecy.

As you begin this study of the book of Daniel, consider the following:

- Why are you engaging in this study of the book of Daniel?
- What have your previous understandings and opinions of prophets, angels, visions, and apocalyptic literature been? Do you go into this study with any preconceived notions? If so, jot them down before reading.
- What do you hope to learn and discern for yourself in this study?
- What are the Babylonian and Persian empires like at this period of our world's history? How is it different to today's world? Similar?

Before each chapter section of this study guide, portions of scripture will be suggested to read ahead of time. If possible, use a Bible that contains the Apocrypha, as well as the 1979 Book of Common Prayer for reference. You may also wish to have a map of the Persian Empire during the Babylonian captivity and Persian Empire. These can be found in the appendix of most study Bibles.

Chapter One: The Kingdom, the Power, and the Glory

This first chapter sets the scene for Daniel and how these writings became part of our canon of scripture. Questions are immediately posed as to the purpose of these stories as well as their meaning to us today:

- Can we read the book of Daniel in a way that is faithful to the historical context yet still be applicable and relevant for our own time and place?

- How do we balance our obligations to God with our responsibilities as citizens?
- Whom do the kingdom, the power, and the glory belong to?
- Are the kingdoms of this world and God's realm separate but equal realities, and is it possible to serve both God and "king"?
- Out of all the generations who have lived and died since the book was written, do we alone matter to God? Who matters to God?

Read Genesis 6:9, Job 42:7–9, Daniel 1:1–21, and Ezekiel 14:12–23

- Ezekiel (14:14) refers to Daniel, Job, and Noah as being models of righteousness. What do these three "characters" have in common that Ezekiel would refer to them in such a way? What is righteousness?

Read "The Prayer of Azariah and The Song of Three Young Men" (also called The Song of the Three Jews), "Susanna," and "Bel and the Dragon." Each can be found in the Apocrypha.

Desueza and Jones review the types of writing that composes the book of Daniel as well as the characteristics of the individuals portrayed in the stories. Comparisons are also made with many other figures in the Hebrew Scriptures.

- Wisdom literature addresses the question, "What does it mean to live a wise life?" How is Daniel characteristic of wisdom literature? How not? What does having wisdom mean to you? What does it mean to be wise when the king's will and God's will stand in conflict with each other?
- What do you imagine when you hear the word "apocalyptic"? What is your understanding of revelation? In what ways are the two similar and/or different?
- What events of our own time are similar to the events described of Daniel's dealings with the Babylonian and Persian kings?

Daniel was written during different periods of exile, destruction, and changes of the Jewish people. After a period of time, it became more and more difficult to maintain one's personal, cultural, and religious practices as the people became assimilated into the Babylonian, then Persian, then Greek world. For a culture to survive, its people must retain their identity, despite the challenges faced in day-to-day life visible all around them. Public sacrifices, the worship of many gods, and the practice of circumcision in a culture that promoted public exercise of mind and (naked) body, are just a few of the societal "norms" faced by the Jews living in exile or back home in Jerusalem. Conquerors define the terms and conditions by which the conquered live.

- What practices today are in conflict with our religious beliefs?
- Where have we seen religious persecution in recent times?
- Where do we see persecution occurring today, locally and globally?
- What are the signs of our times that are similar to what the Jews faced during their exile and return?
- How can we, as a people of God, remain faithful while living in a world dominated by rulers and systems that oppose what we believe God calls us to be?
- If we were to write a supplement to Daniel to describe the world today, what might it read like?

The authors and their interpretation of Daniel see the book as "speaking not only to those who are confronting violent political oppression, but also to those who face the more subtle pressure to placate the rich and the powerful in order to get ahead in the world. The heroes in Daniel model both nonviolent resistance to evil and faithfulness. . . ." Like Daniel's original audience living under economic and political forces that transformed the culture, we too face similar situations. It is a question of faith and what it means to be fully human. How can we take this study of Daniel to be instructive in our own modern culture of exploitation, commercial interests, and the needs of the world today for a just society?

Chapter Two: Which Lord?

Stories form an important role in shaping faith, forming character, and enabling us to see the connection between our lives and God's purpose for the world. Stories capture our imagination and help us visualize the abstract concepts of our world and articulate our faith in real life terms.

- What stories have influenced your faith and life?
- What is the source of your life and hope?
- What stories have been passed down to you from your family, generation to generation? Have they helped give your life meaning? If so, how?
- What stories of your faith community have formed your congregation? How have the challenges, experiences, and celebrations made the congregation what it is today?
- Which do you value more—safety, a comfortable life, success, or God? Which would be the easiest to give up and why? Which would be the most difficult?
- What does a faithful life look like?
- What kinds of temptations do you face today? How do you overcome such temptations? What leads you to succumb to temptations?
- How has God been involved in your life?

Read Daniel 1:1–7 and Genesis 11:1–9

- If history is a story told by the winners, how do the losers keep their identity and their religious faith from being distorted or lost altogether?
- Why are names important?
- How important is it to retain one's language of origin?
- Have you ever named anything, such as a child or pet? Why did you choose the name?

Read Daniel 1:8–21

- When have we seen similar fasts in our time to draw notice to a perceived injustice?
- What other ways do the oppressed act in order to retain their practices and beliefs when persecuted?
- "Prophetic texts associate the gluttony of the rich not simply with insensitivity, but also with the oppressive use of power." Where else have we read this in scripture? Does this continue in the world today?
- Who gives us a vision for today? Who are the prophets of our time?

- Did you receive any cultural experiences from a previous generation? What would you hope to pass on to future generations?
- How do minority populations in your home community maintain their distinctiveness? How do they avoid becoming assimilated?
- How do social groups maintain their identity and avoid becoming irrelevant?

"The book of Daniel portrays God as the one to whom humans owe not only the vision of a better world, but the power to realize that vision" (p. 18). Desueza and Jones challenge us to live a life dedicated to making a difference in the world.

- Read Martin Luther King Jr.'s "I Have a Dream" speech (http://www.americanrhetoric.com/speeches/mlkihaveadream.htm). How is this related to Daniel and his commitment to God?
- When has someone given you an opportunity to model or mentor them?
- How were scribes sources of power? Who has a comparable role in society today?
- Do you ever face the same type of ethical dilemmas faced by Daniel and his friends, as well as the scribes who wrote about such matters?
- Is it possible to obey two masters?

Chapter Three: The Dream of Nebuchadnezzar

Nebuchadnezzar's impossible demand prepares us (the reader) for Daniel's role as a supremely competent interpreter in the coming chapters of the book of Daniel. Dream and omen interpretation were widely practiced in Babylon, and are reminiscent of the stories from Genesis where Joseph was the interpreter of Pharaoh's dreams. Images and identity are often interconnected, even in our world today, whether in dreams or in the messages overtly around us in the public sector.

Read Daniel 2:1–49 and Genesis 40:1–41:57

- When have you had terrifying dreams? Has anything in your life triggered them? Do you go for comfort or explanation afterward? If so, where or to whom?

- Who are the tyrants of the world today? Where do we see those in power terrify their co-workers, subjects, or fellow citizens?
- What happens when tyrants are confronted with the truth and their limits?
- What do the dreams of Nebuchadnezzar and Pharaoh have in common? What do Daniel and Joseph have in common?
- How are Daniel and Joseph able to interpret dreams? How are we able to interpret our own dreams (or those of others)?

Read Daniel 3:1–30

- How do images shape human conceptions (and misconceptions) of God?
- Where is the line between cultivating self-images and worshipping idols?
- What images in our culture do you most identify with? Are there particular images in the media, commercials or advertisements that you are especially vulnerable to? If so, which ones and why?
- How could you submit yourself utterly to the will of God? What would you have to give up? What would you have to change about yourself or your lifestyle?

The stories in Daniel promise that God is faithful to God's people. Even in difficult circumstances of exile, in a pagan place far from the Promised Land, God's people can have hope. It is Yahweh who gives Daniel "favor and compassion" (Daniel 1:9). The story of Shadrach, Meshach, and Abednego in the fiery furnace demonstrates the power of God to defend those who are faithful to God, but there are other issues as well. God will be vindicated—because God is faithful—the story tells us. In the meantime, as we wait for vindication, we must act always in good faith.

- Why are gold, silver, bronze, and iron seen as a contrast to God?
- How does the God of heaven destroy delusions and reshape human lives?
- Are you ever carried away by a sense of your own importance? What causes this and what makes you aware of your behavior?
- What symbols of religion, politics, and power can be found in the world today?

- In what ways does our way of life in the United States depend on obedient "courtiers" and a submissive populace?
- How do you behave when your power (or sense of self) is threatened?
- What is steadfastness? Have you ever exhibited such steadfastness as shown by the three men who refused to bow to Nebuchadnezzar's image?
- Where is the line between prudence and faithlessness in serving God and others?
- What convictions do you have that are worth dying for, if any?
- Can the presence of God be enough when one is facing suffering or death? If so, how?
- "We seek to control others and bend them to our will, and allow ourselves to be tempted by rewards and intimidated by threats." Do you agree or disagree? What examples can you give?

Chapter Four: The Writing on the Wall

Again, the stories in Daniel point to God's sovereignty. God is king over every earthly king, lord over every earthly lord. While Daniel is the main character, he is not the primary focus—God is. Dreams, visions, and supernatural occurrences show us the tension between wealth, power, and injustice. Desueza and Jones state, "When people begin to imagine defying the king, they are already halfway to taking action. The first step to freedom is believing that the tyrant is not almighty and that God alone is sovereign, a claim with serious implications."

Read Psalm 72

- What is the role of a king, ruler, or leader of a nation? For what purpose do they exist?
- Explore recent world events in which local citizens have sought to overthrow tyrants, such as in Tunisia, Egypt, and Libya. Have any of these been grounded in religious fervor? Where is God in these events?
- When have we seen leaders fail? What leads to their downfall? What are the outcomes for the leader and the people?

Read the verses to Hymn 618 in The Hymnal 1982 ("Ye watchers and ye holy ones")

- What is a "holy watcher"?
- What do you believe (or not) about angels?
- The authors refer to Jubilees 4:15–16 (http://www.sacred-texts .com/bib/jub/) and 1 Enoch 15:3–12 (http://www.sacred-texts .com/bib/bep/bep02.htm). How are "watchers" described here?
- Do angels or "watchers" appear today? In what forms?

Read Daniel 4:1–6:28

- When do we view things differently than they really are or how others view them? Give examples. Why do such interpretations differ?
- The authors discuss the imagery and importance of trees in Sumerian and Assyrian literature. Why is this? What do you associate with trees?
- What does it mean to be human? What does it mean to have reason?
- Are there any injustices that occur in our society or world today? What is our responsibility as a Christian in these instances? Do you ever take a stand? If so, what have the consequences been? If not, why not?
- What "objects" do Christians consider holy, and why? Do we lift them up as idols? How do we act when they are desecrated? How do they allow us to approach the divine presence?
- What does the phrase "the handwriting on the wall," mean to you when you hear it in everyday conversation?
- When does religious conviction collide with the good order of society?
- How does your faith make you vulnerable in society? How so? What do you do to defend yourself?
- Is there any part of your faith you'd be willing to give up?
- What is embodied prayer?
- Do you experience daily prayer? If so, why? What does it give you?

The first six chapters of Daniel represent the kind of piety that would have been considered exemplary by the book's audience. These were observant Jews who were faced to participate in syncretizing practices of the upper classes of their people during the Hellenistic reign of Antiochus IV Epiphanes whom can be read about in 1 Maccabees 1:41–43. For these readers, "the retributive justice of the punishment inflicted on Daniel's accusers is obvious."

- What is "retributive justice"? Do we see this occurring in the world today?
- How can accusations eat away at a person or a person's character?
- Where in modern times have we seen the innocent suffer because of decisions in which they had no part?
- Name some minorities throughout history and today whose distinctive cultural and religious practices make them vulnerable to false charges of sedition and treason?
- Do we have any civil laws that conflict with God's law?
- What are the values that shape our culture today? Are they similar or different than in Daniel's time?
- Have you ever been cost a promotion, position, or job because of your values and choices by which you live?
- How do you discern the boundary between religion and culture? Is there a boundary? Should there be?
- One of our Baptismal Promises is to "strive for justice and peace among all people, respecting the dignity of every human being" (BCP, 305). Are we obligated to speak prophetically, calling attention to injustice no matter where it occurred or who committed it? What is the cost for doing so? What is the cost for being silent?

Chapter Five: The Night Visions

The visions in the next chapters of Daniel point to the establishment of the kingdom of God. Scholars generally agree that these chapters were written in the mid–second century BCE to support the Maccabean revolt against Seleucid Syria. Behind the success of the Maccabean revolution (164 BCE) stood the influence of a group called the *chasidim*. The name means "pious ones," or the "godly ones." They were Jews who held fast to the old ways of Judaism. Among the *chasidim* were apocalyptic writers. In Daniel, they use symbols to refer to the foreign powers whose rise and fall mark the different ages of world history.

Read Daniel 7:1–8:27

In Daniel chapters 7 to 12, we read of visions of the future. This is where Daniel begins to take the form of apocalyptic writing, pointing to the end times. Its focus is not on predicting the future, but giving some meaning to present happenings. By explaining past events that led up to a terrible situation, it shows that all along God has permitted everything that takes place and is planning to act soon to rescue God's people.

- Describe the various theories of dreams that you have heard about. Which theory best fits the position taken by Daniel? What position do you hold?
- Apocalyptic literature is grist for various interpretations of the Christian message. Consider what you might make of this kind of literature. What might it mean to those who are living in a situation that does not support one's faith or limits one's freedom? Has anything like this ever happened to you? If not, what would you do if it did?
- How does apocalyptic literature help you understand the end of things?
- What is time?
- Some would say we are living in the end times? What are the signs that give this indication? What do you believe?

What are some of the symbolic meanings of these in the visions? Are these images reminiscent of any other stories in scripture? Look up those passages (such as in Genesis, Ezekiel, Isaiah, and Revelation) and compare and contrast.

- Four winds
- Four beasts (lion, bear, leopard, fourth beast)
- Sea
- Horns
- Thrones
- Fiery flames
- Wheels
- Numbers

Desueza and Jones state, "The entire book of Daniel emphasizes that human power and human beings are temporal and limited." At the conclusion of this book's chapter 5, they say, "The visions in Daniel 7 and 8 teach us that both human beings and God have a role to play in human history." We also get a glimpse of a developing angelology in Jewish tradition.

- What does it mean to be fully human?
- How are we without power, "helpless before political and economic forces over which we have no control"? How can we achieve power? Do we need to?
- Gabriel means "warrior of God." Where does the angel Gabriel appeared in the New Testament? What would Gabriel's message be to us today?
- The Feast Day of St. Michael and All Angels is September 29. Read the lections for this day (http://satucket.com/lectionary/Michael.htm).

Read Psalm 102 and Hymn 363 and Hymn 423 (The Hymnal 1982)

God is described as the "ancient of days," the one who has ruled the earth from its foundations. The vision of the judgment scene (Daniel 7:9) determines the destiny of peoples and the "son of man" comes "with the clouds of heaven." This becomes a pattern for many later apocalyptic works.

- How would you explain the "Ancient One"? The Holy One? Are they the same?
- What makes one holy?
- How is God described in Daniel as well as in the above texts?
- How can you describe God and God's dwelling place? What would your vision of such a place be?

Chapter Six: The End of Time

The concluding chapters of Daniel share other visions in which the history of the world empires is described in symbolic terms. Daniel comes to see that the "many days" are not too far away, for according to the divine timetable, the Kingdom of God is at hand.

Read Daniel 9, Jeremiah 25:11–12, 29:10, and Nehemiah 9

- In the Hebrew, Daniel turns his face toward God to seek obeying the spirit of Jeremiah's prophecy. What is prayer to Daniel?

- Read the "Prayer of Confession" in the Book of Common Prayer (BCP, 360). How is Daniel's prayer similar? How are these similar to Ezra's prayer from Nehemiah?
- What do you believe prayer is?
- What is corporate sin? Are there any specific realities that we must face in regard to destruction or life-denying actions of others?
- What does it mean to ask for forgiveness for things "left undone"?
- Write a prayer of intercession that Daniel might say in today's world.
- What in our world today would some say our behavior makes us responsible?
- Read the "Prayer of Humble Access" (BCP, 337). What prayer of supplication might Daniel say to today's world?
- Do you believe God forgives? If so, why does God forgive?

Bernard Anderson writes in *Understanding the Old Testament, 4th edition* (Prentiss Hall, 1998, 571), "The confidence that history moves inevitably and by prearranged plan toward the Kingdom of God fired the zeal of a small band of Jews, enabling them to act and hope when everything seemed against them." Daniel offered hope to those in exile.

- What is it like to live in exile? Where does exile occur metaphorically and actually today?
- What is your understanding of the concept of Jubilee? Where could we see this enacted in the world today?
- What are the "spoils of war" in our own modern day?
- How can our churches serve as vehicles for forgiveness?
- Who does land belong to? What is meant by public and private land?

Read Daniel 10:1–11:45, Isaiah 6:1–13 and Ezekiel 9:2–7

- How is Daniel like the prophets Isaiah and Ezekiel?
- What is the prototype of a faithful servant of God?
- Read the prayers said at Confirmation (BCP, 418). How are they similar to the calling and strengthening of Daniel and other prophets?

THE BOOK OF DANIEL

- Have you ever felt abandoned by God? How could reading Daniel provide strength and comfort?
- What does it mean to be wise?
- How do we (or those in power) take advantage of existing realities?
- How do you contemplate and confess the sovereignty of God?
- How do you put your beliefs into practice?
- What obligation, if any, do the educated have in advocating for those in exile or those who have no power?
- How does persecution test the faithful? Name some examples.

Read Daniel 12:1–14

Daniel does not mention the Messiah ("Anointed One"), who in the last days would appear as God's agent, either to execute judgment on Israel's oppressors or to rule over God's people in righteousness.

- Compare the visions and term "Son of Man" used by Daniel, Jesus (Mark 13:3–37) and John (Revelation 1:12–20). How are they similar? How are they different?
- Where is God's justice?
- Who do we have that preserves the traditions of the past and present today?
- What would you say to those who would predict that the end times are at hand today?

Concluding thoughts:

- What are the most significant insights you have gleaned from reading the book of Daniel?
- Is Daniel an explanation of past events or for all time?
- As you look to the future, what does the apocalyptic literature suggest to you about what is to come and your understanding of your ministry in the future?
- Which of Daniel's visions challenge you the most?
- How different are you for having engaged in this study?
- What is God calling you to do in light of your study?

Sharon Ely Pearson is the Christian Formation Specialist for Church Publishing Incorporated /Morehouse Education Resources. She lives in Norwalk, Connecticut.

NOTES

1. David F. Ford, "The Bible, the World and the Church I," *The Official Report of the Lambeth Conference 1998,* ed. J. Mark Dyer (Harrisburg, PA: Morehouse, 1999), 332.
2. For my broader understanding of authority, I am indebted to Eugene Kennedy and Sara C. Charles, *Authority: The Most Misunderstood Idea in America* (New York: Free Press, 1997).
3. William Sloane Coffin, *Credo* (Louisville, KY: Westminster John Knox Press, 2003), 156.
4. C. L. Seow, *Daniel* (Louisville, KY: Westminster John Knox, 2003), 6.
5. Walter Brueggemann, *Theology of the Old Testament* (Minneapolis: Fortress, 1997), 699.
6. Seow, *Daniel,* 69.
7. Daniel L. Smith-Christopher, "The Book of Daniel," *The New Interpreter's Bible* (Nashville: Abingdon, 1996), 7: 84.
8. Seow, *Daniel,* 90.
9. This insight comes from Filipino activist Melba Padilla Maggay's book *Transforming Society. Reflections on the Kingdom and Politics,* 2nd ed. (Quezon City, Philippines: Institute for Studies in Asian Church and Culture, 2004), 98.
10. Bill Wylie Kellermann, "Bill, the Bible, and the Seminary Underground," in *Radical Christian and Exemplary Lawyer,* ed. Andrew W. McThenia (Grand Rapids, MI: Eerdmans: 1995), 68.

CONTINUING THE CONVERSATION: SUGGESTIONS FOR FURTHER READING

For an excellent study Bible that includes the Greek additions to Daniel ("The Prayer of Azariah," "The Song of the Three Jews," "Susanna," and "Bel and the Dragon") as well as 1 and 2 Maccabees, see *The Access Bible: New Revised Standard Version with the Apocryphal/Deuterocanonical Books,* ed. Gail R. O'Day and David Petersen (Oxford and New York: Oxford University Press, 1999).

Knowing biblical history helps the book of Daniel to come alive. One interesting and accessible introduction to the period when Daniel was written is Leonard J. Greenspoon, "Between Alexandria and Antioch: Jews and Judaism in the Hellenistic Period," in *The Oxford History of the Biblical World,* ed. Michael D. Coogan (Oxford: Oxford University Press, 1998), 317–51. For a wealth of cultural and historical background on the book of Daniel, see Sharon Pace, *Daniel,* Smyth & Helwys Bible Commentary (Macon, GA: Smyth & Helwys, 2008). For a fascinating collection of historical information related to the story of Nebuchadnezzar's madness, see Matthias Henze, *The Madness of King Nebuchadnezzar: The Ancient Near Eastern Origins and Early History of Interpretation of Daniel 4,* Supplements to the Journal for the Study of Judaism 61 (Leiden: Brill, 1999).

For an introduction to the role that the scribes played in Jewish society, see Richard A. Horsley, *Revolt of the Scribes: Resistance and Apocalyptic Origins* (Minneapolis: Fortress, 2010). Horsley explores the relationship between the scribes' resistance to imperial rule and the many apocalyptic books that were written during the late Hellenistic and early Roman periods.

In Daniel, as in many books of the Bible, economic and social policies are religious issues. Most of the biblical books were written during times when Israel was living under economic and social structures imposed by foreign kings. For a profound discussion of the Bible's various responses to this challenge, see Wes Howard-Brook, *"Come Out, My People!": God's Call out of Empire in the Bible and Beyond* (Maryknoll, NY: Orbis Books, 2010).

Like many rulers past and present, Antiochus IV Epiphanes imposed his will through acts of brutality and terror as well as by economic and political manipulation. The Maccabees chose to resist him with violence; the book of Daniel advocates nonviolent resistance instead. For an interpretation that pays particular attention to Daniel's response to violence in all its forms, see Daniel L. Smith-Christopher, "The Book of Daniel," in *The New Interpreter's Bible* (Nashville: Abingdon, 1996), 7:17–152.

Two engaging short commentaries on Daniel are C. L. Seow, *Daniel* (Louisville, KY: Westminster John Knox, 2003) and Danna Nolan Fewell, *Circle of Sovereignty: Plotting Politics in the Book of Daniel* (Nashville: Abingdon, 1991). Seow's commentary is especially noteworthy for his perceptive treatment of theological questions and for his vivid account on p. 76 of the story of Babylon's fall. Of special interest in Fewell's commentary is her chapter "Your Father the King," a literary and psychological interpretation of Belshazzar's feast.

The tales about Daniel and his friends invite us to explore the connections between our own stories and the divine story. For a classic discussion of the interweaving of personal stories, biblical stories, and liturgy, see Herbert Anderson and Edward Foley, *Mighty Stories, Dangerous Rituals: Weaving Together the Human and the Divine* (San Francisco: Jossey-Bass, 1998).

ABOUT THE AUTHORS

Edmond F. Desueza is Priest in Charge at the Church of the Good Shepherd/La Iglesia del Buen Pastor in Newburgh, New York. He studied theology at the Episcopal Seminary in Haiti and earned a doctorate in law at the Autonomous University of Santo Domingo in the Dominican Republic. He has lived and worked in a variety of countries, serving as a parish priest and founding night schools for adult workers in the Dominican Republic, establishing programs for refugees and for the rural and urban poor in Central America, and, as Executive Secretary, guiding the formation of the Episcopal Province of the Caribbean. He has published a number of articles in both Spanish and English and serves as a keynote speaker at workshops and conferences throughout the U.S., the Caribbean, and Central America.

Judith Jones is Associate Professor of Religion at Wartburg College and Priest in Charge at St. Andrew's Episcopal Church in Waverly, Iowa. She earned an MDiv from Princeton Theological Seminary, a certificate in Anglican Studies from The School of Theology at the University of the South, and a PhD in Biblical Studies from Emory University. As the Millennium Development Goal coordinator for the Diocese of Iowa, she helps oversee the awarding of minigrants for projects that alleviate poverty and foster human dignity and community development. Every other year she takes a group of students to the Dominican Republic to work in an impoverished community and reflect critically on the church's responsibility to do justice.